IRELAND AFTER THE END OF WESTERN CIVILISATION

DESMOND FENNELL

ATHOL BOOKS
WWW.ATHOLBOOKS.ORG

BOOKS BY DESMOND FENNELL SINCE 1990

Bloomsway: A Day in the Life of Dublin (1990)

Whatever You Say, Say Nothing: Why Seamus Heaney Is No.1 (pamphlet, 1991)

Heresy: The Battle of Ideas in Modern Ireland (1993)

Dreams of Oranges: An Eyewitness Account of the Fall of Communist East Germany (1996)

Uncertain Dawn: Hiroshima and the Beginning of Postwestern Civilisation (1996)

The Postwestern Condition: Between Chaos and Civilisation (1999)

The Turning Point: My Sweden Year and After (2001)

The Revision of European History (2003)

Cutting to the Point: Essays and Objections 1994-2003 (2003)

Savvy and the Preaching of the Gospel (pamphlet, 2003)

About Behaving Normally in Abnormal Circumstances (2007)

Ireland after the End of Western Civilisation
by
Desmond Fennell
ISBN: 978 08034 120 1
2009
Athol Books

Orders:
athol-st@atholbooks.org

Athol Books, PO Box 339, Belfast, BT12 4GQ

Contents

Preface	5
The Second American Revolution and the Sense Famine in the West	7
Ireland's Call	27
A Public Ritual Well Performed	30
Totalitarianism Domesticated	34
The New Arrivals among the Statues	41
John Waters Gets It Almost Right	46
An Irish *Camino de Santiago*	51
Where Is the European Union Heading?	54
The Emptying Churches of Irish Catholicism	60
The Ghost of Europe	68
The Illegible Treaty of Lisbon	69
Goodbye to Terry Keane	71
The Campaigns Rage	75
Sorting Out Art in Dublin	78
Irish Times and Irish People	84
Dundrum's New Cathedral	91
The No to Lisbon	97
Postscript	98
Afterthought	100
Index	101

*To Enrico, Barbara,
Peppe, Gabi, Enrica, Piero,
Alice, Kristine, Carlo,
with good memories
and thanks*

Preface

During the nine and a half years I spent in Italy, from autumn 1997 to spring 2007, most of my thinking and writing was an attempt to understand the present condition of the western world. That it had passed out of European or western civilisation was an insight I had gained in two long visits to the USA in the mid-1990s. But that merely opened the question as to where and how the West was now.

I was trying to understand the western age I was living in, so that I could spend the remainder of my time on earth seeing, rather than not seeing. Back in the 1960s I had read that the French writer Camus had said that understanding the age one lived in was a sufficient achievement for a man in his lifetime. That encouraged me by suggesting that in my own querying fascination with the age I lived in – Camus could not be the only trier – I was far from being alone. It goes without saying that the understanding I was seeking was not the sort of thing that the age itself – or any age – supplies.

Although its public explanatory agencies purport to be telling contemporaries how things are and why, they are of necessity not doing so. Of necessity, partly because they have not devoted great effort to discovering the truth of the matter, but mainly because they are supplying explanations that serve powerful interests rather than the truth. And since part of serving powerful interests is to maintain tranquillity of minds and order on the streets, that, far from being entirely a bad thing, has the beneficial effect of preventing the lives of most people from being 'nasty, brutish and short'.

In some of the books I wrote while in Italy, I had made jabs at comprehension in the form of essays, long and short, and epigrams, about one aspect or other of the age. Returned to Ireland in 2007, I found myself, over the best part of a year, attempting to write a summary essay and publishing successive versions of it on my website. Now, at the beginning of May 2008, with Brian Cowen about to become Taoiseach, I feel it is more or less adequate. In its final form, it opens this book.

While presenting an existing problematic state of affairs, it also indicates the necessary remedy. In view of this, it is followed by a short essay, 'Ireland's Call', in which during those same months I had sketched out how thoughtful and concerned Irishmen might contribute to that remedy. As an intellectual procedure, this was a kind of repeat, only with a broader focus, of what I had done in the years 1969-72 with regard to the dual problem of the Irish language revival and the Gaeltacht and the problem of Northern Ireland: a fresh, unideological analysis followed by a proposal of a new approach. There were two main differences. The problematic situation I was now dealing with had not previously been recognised as such; and the remedial enterprise in which I was proposing some Irishmen might play a leading role, namely, the building of a new civilisation, was unlikely because of its vast and speculative quality to get immediately under way. It seemed nevertheless, for the reasons I give in that short piece, worth proposing it.

Believing that I had completed the task I had set myself in the mid-1990s, I was wondering what to do next. Had the moment finally arrived to join the men and boys who fish in the canal? But willy-nilly I found myself drawing benefit, daily, from the overall view of things western that I had won. I was seeing particular things around me, in Ireland and elsewhere, with greater clarity than before. The result was that, not entirely happily but feeling compelled, I started writing down what I was seeing afresh, and the thoughts it gave rise to. And I continued doing so. These addenda to the initial essay form the remainder of the book.

Maynooth
5 May 2008

The Second American Revolution and the Sense Famine in the West

The prevalent understanding of the recent and contemporary history of the West contains three serious errors. In the first place, we have believed that some of the chief collective actors in this western age – specifically, the Americans and their close allies – have in respect of the moral quality of their intentions and behaviour *not* been made up of the standard human mix. Furthermore, we have believed that these chief actors have *not* tended to act either in ways characteristic of the age, or in ways that have precedents in past history.

Rather than leave these three implausible beliefs to future historians to correct, I have disbelieved them and, in their absence, taken a fresh look at the history of the West in the past eighty years and at the state of affairs which has emerged from it.

As a result, I argue, first, *that the West's present socio-ethical system is a utopian experiment, originating in and emanating from the USA, and based on post-European rules of behaviour.* Second, *that in those respects, its origin apart, it is similar to the Soviet Russian experiment.* Third, *that our system's continuing existence depends, not on any sense it makes to westerners, but merely on the constant increase of the power to buy things and do things which it has been providing to states and consumers.* And finally, *that when that increase ceases, it will dissolve into violent social chaos, leaving the task of building the widely desired post-European civilisation to a future generation.*

To understand how all this is indeed the case, it is necessary to recognise the fact, context, nature and effect of the Second American Revolution.

1

> The contemporary West is built not on Auschwitz and Treblinka to which we have said 'No', but on Hiroshima and Nagasaki to which we have said 'Yes'.
> *The Postwestern Condition: Between Chaos and Civilisation* (1993) p79.

If we recognise that the Second American Revolution began in 1933, simultaneously with the German Revolution and during the latter phase of the Russian Revolution, many aspects of life in the West today are clarified. In particular, light is thrown on an unintended result of that American revolution: the pervasive senselessness of western life that has been made bearable only by the constant increase of the power to buy and do things which has characterised the last half-century.[1]

The fact that the transformation of the United States between 1933 and the early 1970s has not generally been called a revolution takes nothing from the fact that it was indeed that. A similar failure of recognition occurred with regard to the long-drawn-out replacement of the republic by one-man rule in ancient Rome. Although it was in fact a revolution, it was not recognised as such, and called that, until Ronald Syme's book *The Roman Revolution*, published in 1939, made the term current.

In both instances, the forces that effected the revolution wished to give the impression that the constitution had not been overturned, but that the public business continued to be conducted within the inherited framework, only better. In addition, in the American case, American exceptionalism was operative. According to this mythical way of seeing things, a revolution was unthinkable because the American Constitution was an act of collective virtue that had broken with history, stood outside history, and was the condition of existence of the USA. As previously in the Roman case, so, too, in this case: history writing has been compliant with the revolutionaries. (A book published in 1935, E. T. Colton's *Four Patterns of Revolution: Communist U.S.S.R., Fascist Italy, Nazi Germany, New Deal America*, has remained a curiosity of its time.)

---

[1] This is an amended and extended version of the essay under the same title which appeared in *Church & State* (Cork), Nos. 92, 93, 2008.

In the minds of their idealistic activists and in fact, those three twentieth-century revolutions, Russian, German and American, largely shared a common nature and purpose with previous revolutions in the history of Europe and Europe Overseas. Each of them took possession of a nation's central government and by unconstitutional action increased its power. Using that augmented power, they imposed a new order and a new worldview, while empowering those who were likely – by their nature or in response to their empowerment – to support the new order, and disempowering opponents, domestic or foreign.

In one important aspect, however, these three revolutions differed from those that had preceded them and, indeed, from the Irish and Italian revolutions in the same century. They broke with the tacit common constitution of European nations which prescribed that political, including military, action must respect – or after a transgression re-assert – the essential ethical and customary rules of European (*alias* western) civilisation. Occasionally, a revolutionary power had contravened that normative framework or – as in the French Revolution – for a time proclaimed new rules. But never had a revolution invalidated the framework by enduringly establishing new rules in place of essential rules of European civilisation.

The Russian and American revolutions did this, and it was evident that the German revolution would have done so had it survived. All three declared and implemented new rules of behaviour in place of essential European rules, including many which Christianity had long preached as God's rules. They thereby launched experimental systems of human living not previously attempted by Europeans at home or overseas.[2]

The German and Russian systems, which for a short and a long period, respectively, operated in much of Europe, have perished. Only that resulting from the Second American Revolution – the system in which we now live in the West – remains. In order to have a clear view of what its departure from European civilisation amounted

---

[2] Between 1890 and the 1920s, a growing number of European artists had rejected the European rules for the arts and experimented with new forms. They had thus prefigured in the artistic field what these revolutionary rulers now did with regard to the European rules for human behaviour. Retrospectively seen, those artists resembled the animals whose anomalous behaviour indicates and forecasts an approaching earthquake.

to, it is useful to recall what a civilisation is, and western civilisation in particular.³

What a civilisation is, essentially

A civilisation is essentially a grounded hierarchy of values and rules covering all of life and making sense, which a community's rulers and ruled subscribe to over a long period. 'Over a long period' (unless a catastrophe overwhelms it) because the community is motivated to keep reproducing itself by the sense, and therefore goodness, that it finds in its framework for life.

The rules to which it subscribes cover all behaviour from the maintenance of the state and communication with the supernatural to international relations in peace and war and dealings among persons and between men and women. The rules derive hierarchically from the hierarchy of values. This dual hierarchy – representing the greater or lesser importance to the community of the elements so arranged – is 'grounded' in the sense that there are interconnected reasons, understood or intuited by the community, for the presence in it of those values and rules and for their order of ranking. Some of the rules are adjustable or replaceable as the centuries pass and circumstances and mentalities change. The essential rules are those whose continuous acceptance is necessary for the civilisation to remain itself. They form its defining core.

Constructed in western Europe by Latin, Germanic and Celtic Christians, western civilisation had crossed the Atlantic and other seas and had lasted almost a thousand years. Among its essential rules were the following:

The West is a Christian civilisation of Christian nations. Its divinity is the Christian God. Whether on religious grounds or for secular motives, national and international law generally subscribe to the Christian principles of interpersonal and international behaviour. Connection with the West's Roman-Greek-Judaic roots is maintained through the educational system and educated public discourse. An

---

³ For some further treatment of the matters arising here, see my 'The West's Campaign for Mastery of the World' in *Irish Political Review*, August 2003 and in my *Cutting to the Point: Essays and Objections* 1994-2003, Dublin: The Liffey Press, 2003. For the Second American Revolution, see also my *The Postwestern Condition*, London: Minerva Press, 1999, pp.30-35 and *The Revision of European History*, Belfast: Athol Books, 2003, pp. 92-7 .

educated man knows Latin. Art is work which has a formal crafted beauty. Frugality and chastity are admirable virtues. Reason takes precedence over feeling and desire. Private property is protected by law. Massacre is grievously wrong and strictly forbidden. Sexual relations are legitimate only in the monogamous betrothal and marriage of man and woman. Homosexual relations are unnatural and abhorrent. Abortion is a heinous crime, pornography a degrading evil that must be denied circulation. Adults do not foist sexual awareness on children. A girl who bears a child without a committed father is a disgrace. Human nudity and bodily intimacies are not for public display, but nudity may be represented decorously in art. Men's work and women's work are different. Men have authority and legal precedence over women; they accord women social pre-eminence and physical protection. Age has authority over youth.

Such were some of the essential rules which, in combination with others, made sense to our ancestors for nearly a thousand years.

In a process that began at the end of World War II, the West's democratic rulers, led by those of the USA, rejected many of the essential rules of western civilisation and introduced new rules in place of the rejected ones. This process was part of, or derived transatlantically from, the Second American Revolution. The rulers worked in collaboration with late arrivals on the western scene: the 'new' or 'left-'liberals.

These utopian idealists (known in Ireland since the 1970s as 'the Dublin liberals') had a prehistory in American 'progressivism'. Under the name 'liberals' they first rose to prominence in the 1930s in the USA. Unlike their classical-liberal predecessors in Europe and the USA (in Ireland, the liberals who took their lead from Daniel O'Connell and who drafted our Constitutions after Independence) these fundamentalists wanted a powerful and active state – a 'Big State' as a slogan went – intervening to shape the lives of people for their good.

The revolution gets under way

President Franklin D. Roosevelt, with the support of the Democratic Party, brought the left-liberals to power. Elected in 1932 in the midst of the Great Depression, Roosevelt was convinced that their 'Big State' project was the best means of tackling its dire economic consequences. His New Deal programme, inspired in part by Mussolini's Italy and Stalin's Russia, transferred powers from the states to the federal government and extended the range of government action. Its immediate purpose was to liberate millions of citizens from unemployment and poverty, but it impinged on all spheres of American public life, including the arts. Its thrust, in short, in the public domain, was 'totalitarian', in the original and basic meaning of that word.[4]

When twelve New Deal measures were declared unconstitutional by the Supreme Court, Roosevelt threatened to appoint extra judges who would approve them. Eventually, with the help of left-liberal judges appointed to fill vacancies, the Court was rendered compliant. Between 1937 and 1946, it reversed thirty-two of its earlier interpretations of the Constitution, extending back over a period of 150 years. In effect, therefore, the Supreme Court presented the revolutionary government with a new Constitution tailored to its needs. In 1940, in disregard of American precedent, Roosevelt was elected President for a third term. (Later, he would seek and win election for a fourth term, and like his German revolutionary counterpart, whose period in power coincided with his, die in office.)

The Big State thus consolidated, and reinforced by emergency powers, made war on and defeated America's two main rivals, Germany and Japan. In respect of power directed outwards, it reached its apogee with the manufacture of the atomic bomb, the use of this weapon against two Japanese cities, and the subsequent official justification of the resulting massacres; in part immediate, but in greater part occurring subsequently as a result of radioactive radiation.

This justification, besides establishing the American state as the first 'superpower', had several weighty implications, two of them retrospective. It legitimised all the deliberate massacres of civilians by American and British aerial bombing during World War II. From the reference in the American Declaration of Independence to 'the

---

[4] When the word emerged in Mussolini's Italy in the 1920s, it denoted a state which - in contradistinction to the previous classical-liberal state – involved itself authoritatively, in tandem with a non-religious teaching authority, in all aspects of the citizens' lives. As the twentieth century progressed, those became common features of all western states. But American exceptionalism, extending its exceptional collective virtue to embrace allies with similar constitutions, denied with imperative effect that anything characteristic of non-liberal-democratic states could be replicated in liberal democracies. So as the liberal democracies engaged in 'totalitarian' practice, they reserved the t-word for non-liberal-democratic states that did likewise.

merciless Indian savages, whose known rules of warfare is an undistinguished destruction of all ages, sexes and conditions' it withdrew the word 'savages'. With immediate effect, it licensed the American state, and by extension its British and French allies, to construct thousands of similar, but more powerful weapons of massacre. Finally, with direct bearing on the revolution in progress, it sent a signal to the fundamentalist liberals about the state they had worked to create; namely, that it was likely to approve those elements of their programme which rejected other core rules of western civilisation.

The general aim of their programme – given the backing of a powerful, active state – was to bring about, by pedagogical, legislative, financial and scientific means, a perfect human condition. For that purpose, first, there must be an end to the tacit recognition of the Christian religion as America's 'national' religion, and to the consequent role of Christian morality as a determinant of behavioural rules. Second, categories of citizens who were legally or otherwise unequal must be raised or lowered to legal equality, so as to bring about a fraternity of individuals, equal in law and in their treatment by their fellows. Third, all citizens must have access to education and health services and be equipped with buying power. And finally, with due regard to the rights of others, the desires of individuals must be recognised as rights and realised as far as possible.

Implicit in that programme were Black civil rights and radical feminism; normalisation of homosexuals and of unmarried mothers and their offspring; political and financial empowerment of young people; maximal facilitation of the physically deficient; invalidation of intrinsic personal authority such as that possessed by clergy, men, parents, teachers and the aged; ample social welfare; unshackling of sex and of pornography of all kinds; legalisation of abortion; and a blank cheque for science. Implicit, too, and duly advocated by the liberals, were a collection of consequent behavioural rules that ran counter to essential European rules, traditional in the USA, which they deemed oppressive or unjust.

The culmination of the revolution

Without invalidation of the West's core rules, the liberal programme had made some progress during the New Deal years and, even more, during the war years almost to their end. But the main work remained to be done. In the remaining Truman years, and through the 1950s, while the liberal party continued to preach its fundamentalist doctrines, conservative opposition prevented further practical progress. The breakthrough came, and the revolution entered its culminating phase, when, at the end of the 1950s and in the following decade, the US government and manufacturing industry needed urgently to increase consumption, with its dual yield of revenue and profit.

The government, already spending heavily to wage the Cold War, was now faced with manufacturing scores of space satellites and thousands more of long-range missiles and nuclear warheads; putting a man on the moon; and paying the rising costs of war in Vietnam. Industries making consumer goods, having greatly raised their productivity by the use of automation and computers, were producing in excess of market demand. Government and manufacturing industry, jointly, perceived in the unfulfilled parts of the liberal agenda the means of greatly increasing consumption.

From the 1960s the American state began endorsing that agenda selectively through Supreme Court rulings, by legislation, and administratively. The state's totalitarian quality, considerable in the public sphere, increased greatly as it imposed new norms of virtuous thought and behaviour on individuals and families, and on educators and employers. Prominent universities played a supporting role.

In the Johnson years, 1963-9, under a liberal President, the revolution celebrated its carnival and launched a rocket against western civilisation into the Nixon 70s, where it exploded on the campuses. In the *Partisan Review* for Winter 1967, Susan Sontag, high-priestess of the American intelligentsia, set the tone for these historically decisive years with the following ringing phrases:

> "If America is the culmination of the Western white civilisation, as everyone from the Left to the Right declares, then there must be something terribly wrong with Western white civilisation…. The truth is that Mozart, Pascal, Boolean algebra, Shakespeare, parliamentary government, baroque churches, Newton, the emancipation of women, Kant, Marx, Balanchine ballets, et al., don't redeem what this particular civilisation has wrought upon the world. The white race *is* the cancer of history."

The teachers of the post-western, liberal rules of correct behaviour came to function, collectively, as a sort of secular state church or informal, doctrinally paramount 'Party'. Henceforth, regardless of which political party was in government, this collective would retain its pre-eminent teaching status.

Given the ending of tacit recognition of the Christian clergy as the supreme extra-Constitutional body teaching ethical rules to the state and the citizens, this was a logical development: a substitute ethical teaching body was called for. And indeed, its emergence brought the USA into line with the practice in other twentieth-century revolutionary states, such as Russia and Germany, where the Christian clergy had been replaced by a supreme Party that defined good and evil. But American exceptionalism, extended to embrace allies with similar constitutions, excluded that anything characteristic of non-liberal-democratic states could be replicated in the US or in other liberal democracies. So another clash occurred between theory and reality: an informal equivalent of the teaching 'Party' did in fact come into being in the US, and later spawned similar bodies in Western Europe. For convenience of the narrative it must have a name. And since its role had to do with defining correct thought and behaviour, to call it the liberal 'Correctorate' seems appropriate.

The formation of this state-liberal system was a case of ambitious political power, and a new ideal vision of the good life, working together towards their distinct objectives. A phenomenon known to history, it operates like this. Rulers who wish to increase their power regardless of the rules, while continuing to rank as virtuous, find substantial common cause with innovative idealists who want society reshaped by new rules that empower people. The rulers increase their political power by enacting the idealists' new rules to their own advantage, while the idealists celebrate them as enlightened and virtuous rulers. The idealists end up powerful in a semblance of their envisioned life that has been tailored to suit the rulers' interests. (In this particular instance, the rulers' interests required, both among individuals and as between swathes of the citizen body, an inequality of living conditions, education and political influence as extreme as in Communist Russia, along with a capitalist inequality of financial power.)

The construction of consumerism

The principal preaching space allotted to the liberals was in the mass media, including films, which they came to dominate pedagogically. (An important secondary podium was the humanities faculties of the universities.) But their pedagogical dominance of the mass media was dependent on, and shared with, business big and small, inasmuch as these same media were the principal public space where business paid to advertise its goods-for-sale.

The advertisers of goods-for-sale were, for business reasons, in substantial agreement with the social and ethical doctrines of the liberal reformers. On this account, and because their advertising campaigns, like the liberals' teaching, amounted to telling people how they should act, live and be – much of it, for example, had to do with personal body care – they de facto formed part of the state-licensed Correctorate. Thus a conjunction of all the interests involved made up that state-liberal system, with ethical, economic, technological and political dimensions, which we call 'consumerism'. It was a new word employed to designate the system of mass consumption, based on the socio-ethical principles of left-liberalism, which took shape in the 1960s and 70s.

It worked this way. The hybrid Correctorate and its supporting legislation issued rulings and exhortations which promoted material and sexual consumption with a good conscience, rather than the previously inculcated virtuous restraint. Advancing science, and military technology by its offshoots, supplied a never-ending array of new, empowering tools to buy. Buying potential and activity were maximised through payments by the state to the poorer citizens, encouragement of all women and teenagers to earn money, incomes constantly rising, goods promotion by television and radio in every home, and the prolongation of active individual life by advances in medicine. Thus mass consumption, material and sexual, became the contemporary equivalent of medieval mass labour in the fields. Together with the instigation, nourishment and exploitation of it under both forms, it constituted the main motor of the economy, society and the state.

Powerful as instigation was the Correctorate's promise that by thinking, consuming, and otherwise acting, in accordance with its exhortations, the legally equalised consumers would individually attain enlightenment and righteousness, ability to do more and more things ethically, lives ever more lasting, and the sensual satisfaction that was everyone's due. All in all, it was, and remains, the culminating realisation of the centuries-old drive by Europeans to acquire, collectively and individually, ever greater ethical power, in the sense of *ability to do more things and bigger things, including things previously illicit, and be justified*.[5]

Consumerism spreads to Western Europe

In London's *Sunday Times*, 21 October 1962, Maurice Wiggins wrote: 'Freedom of speech includes the temporarily unfashionable freedom to express a certain scepticism of liberal shibboleths.' 'Every little authoritarian these days pays lip-service to liberal ideals...' wrote Judith Pakenham in the London *Spectator*, 18 January 1963. The liberals they were talking about were clearly not the Liberals of earlier British history; they were using the word in the new American sense which was to become its normal usage in English-speaking countries. In the 1960s, pressure from the USA via London began the imposition of the new state-liberal system in America's West European satellites.

The aim of the American rulers was to widen the area of maximal money yield and to counter, with a display of permissiveness and prosperity, the communist indoctrination of Eastern Europe. In each West European state, successively, elements of the increasingly well-financed mass media adopted and spearheaded the new ethical doctrines; a national correctorate took shape; the media as a whole conformed; and the rulers, in varying degrees, gave legal force to the new teachings and placed correctors at key points in the state administration.

From the late 1960s onwards, in North America and Western Europe, the national liberal correctorates functioned much as the national communist parties in the Soviet satellites, except in one respect. Whereas the leading doctrinal role of the communist parties in the 'people's democracies' was constitutionally formalised, that of the liberal correctorates was exercised, with tacit state approval, extra-constitutionally, as a matter of fact. So while the former functioned as commanding authority in the respective multi-party

---

[5] As a functioning system, consumerism provided the basis on which the American economic doctrine and practice called 'neoliberalism', with its attendant programme of 'globalisation', would subsequently – with some practical corrections – be built.

parliaments and in society generally, the latter secured conformity partly through the actions of correctors installed in the state bureaucracy, partly by manipulating public opinion so as to influence the decisions of governments, political parties and other institutions. Through the mass media the correctorates allocated public honour, hounding or silencing to significant groups in parliaments and civil society, and to significant writings, speeches and individuals.

As in the communist countries the word 'socialist' was made in the prevalent language to connote 'good', so, in the English-speaking countries, with 'liberal', in the language of citizens who ranked as right-thinking. Conversely, the negative connotation of the ideological terms 'right' and 'right-wing' in the communist East was reproduced in the prevalent discourse of the (left-) liberal West. Frequently in the 1960s, and to a degree in the 1970s, serious talk of 'revolution' had occurred in the political discourse of western radicals. Gradually, as a tacit signal that in the West, as in the East, a definitive revolution had already taken place, that word passed out of politics into commercial advertising, where it served in the promotion of new soap powders or face creams.

In Europe the national correctorates also collaborated with the liberal party in the central administration of the European Community. While these bureaucrats worked to ensure that Community directives and regulations conformed in relevant matters to liberal principles, the national correctorates lauded such measures and insisted on their meticulous implementation in the member states. Similar collaboration, within the Community and the subsequent Union, worked against any political party that deviated notably from liberal orthodoxy holding power in a national government.

The net result, with regard to rules to live by, is that a collection of non-European rules, combined with some surviving European rules, has become the reigning and widely accepted system of do's, don'ts and do-as-you-likes of North America and much of Europe, Ireland centrally included.

2

> There were whispered arguments between our parents while we watched TV - arguments about changing the rules, we gathered, that applied to all of us, the dads and moms as well as the kids...
> Naomi Wolf in *Promiscuities* (1997) on San Francisco in 1970.

A new civilisation can replace an older one on the same ground; history, again, shows instances of that. But this new collection of values and rules is not a case of that. It does not constitute a new civilisation because it lacks the *sine qua non* of a civilisation: it does not make sense to the human collective it is presented to and imposed on, thereby ensuring emotional attachment to it and durability. Thrown together to promote justice, virtue, consumption and power, its hybrid sponsors treated overall sense as superfluous. The result was inevitable. The collection constitutes, like its Soviet counterpart, a theoretical experiment not shaped by combined human instinct, reason and experience. The framework of a wealthy, senseless, state-liberal system, it is life-thwarting, and will, when the growing money force that holds it in being stops growing, prove disastrous.

The absence of sense is immediately evident at the level of the rules. Indeed, by the simple fact that these do not present a grounded hierarchy covering all of life they *cannot* make sense as a framework for living. For a start, they lack a supreme value (lawgiver, virtue or venerated moral inheritance) from which subordinate values and their attendant rules might be derived in descending order of importance to cover all of life. Thus *ipso facto* the rules lack both the validating and the rational grounding which such derivation could provide.

Floating therefore unanchored, assembled pell-mell over the past half-century, the new rules comprise qualitatively undifferentiated do's and don'ts for parts of life and virtual do-as-you-likes for other parts. Among the do's and don'ts, the latter predominate. They are taught much as if the things *not* to do when driving a car were to be imparted without distinguishing in order of importance between failing to glance regularly at the rear-view mirror, passing on the inside, driving on the wrong side of the road, and starting in second gear; that is to say, in a senseless manner, useless to the would-be driver.

The new rules to live by

Take a random array of don'ts as taught and administered by the Correctorate. No intelligible ranking of incorrectness is indicated as between don't kill civilians with non-aerial bombs, don't be fat or speak badly of Jews or urge that a law should reflect Christian morality; don't be smelly or invade another country without the authority of the United Nations or smoke in an enclosed public space or say that homosexuality is a perversion or 'deny the Holocaust'; don't torture prisoners, pollute a river, ban pornography, treat a woman as a sex-object, prevent her having an abortion or restrict what adults read, view, say, write or think; and don't, if a man, hit your wife or pursue a female in the office.

Leave aside the contradictions in that sample. Because the consumers do not have available a grounded exposition by the Correctorate of which of these incorrectnesses is gravely, less gravely or only somewhat incorrect, they must perforce try to gauge this from the Correctorate's reactions or non-reactions to incorrectnesses as they occur. And the teaching thus delivered is bafflingly dual.

On the one hand, it is to the effect that all behaviours or thoughts forbidden by the Correctorate are, for a variety of variously grounded reasons, very grave. On the other hand, the same teaching indicates – read the newspapers – that the gravity of many incorrectnesses is greater, lesser or cancelled, depending on who commits them and why; or if there are victims, on which nation, creed, party or sex they belong to. Inevitably, the conclusion drawn by the consumers is also dual. It is that all the Correctorate's don't rules are of more or less equal importance, and are in practice not really rules.

Much the same would appear if we were to look at a bunch of the do's. In passing, for the plight of young mothers is special, note the particular array of unranked obligations that falls on them if their behaviour is to be correct. Widely broadcast do's of equal imperativeness exhort them to meticulous body care, paid employment, personal assertiveness, vigilant child-rearing in person or by delegation, diligent participation in the consumerist good life, and successfully orgasmic sexual intercourse.

The virtual do-as-you-likes which operate alongside the do's and don'ts are 'virtual' in the sense that the positive rules they contain are so minimal as to leave caprice or desire substantially in command. They deal with areas of human behaviour which western civilisation, as other civilisations, subjected to comprehensive positive rules. In the Correctorate's teaching, virtual do-as-you-likes operate for art in all its forms, for official killing in righteous wars, as for dress, dancing, social manners, propriety of speech, modes of personal address, and relations with the supernatural insofar as these are not declared absurd. A special do-as-you-like applies to the behaviour of the state of Israel.

In all human communities, for the most serious of reasons including collective survival, the use of the human reproductive organs has been subjected to strict and intelligibly grounded rules. Note, by contrast, the Correctorate's rule: provided that minors and adults use their reproductive organs separately, that if more than one user is involved there is mutual consent, and that a condom is employed unless conception is intended, do as you like in private or, in public, to gratify a paying audience.

Reactions to the senselessness

It is not simply that this chaos of rules can be seen on examination not to make sense as a framework for living. It is also *experienced as senselessness* by us white westerners who are required to live by it. For the most part, we experience it as senselessness unreflectively, in that depth of our being where countless generations of human beings before us have trained us by heredity to assess – in a combined act of reason, feeling and intuition – any presentation purporting to be a framework for life. And that encounter with senselessness, when our minds and hearts are seeking sense, sends distress, a pain of soul, pressing into our consciousness. To be precise, we white westerners find that consciousness of this life framework which we have been given for living in is accompanied by pain in our souls. Nothing more natural, then, than that we should want, as individuals, to annul that pain and, collectively, feel little desire to reproduce this white western life.

Sensitive young people, on the threshold of life, are particularly attentive to the framework of rules presented to them. Little wonder then that many of these, over the past half-century, have found and practised various methods of annulling the pain. Some of them, females more often than males, do so by superficial self-injury with a sharp knife, in an effort to manage the pain by transferring it from soul to body. More commonly, male and female, they seek the desired annulment, recurrently, through annihilation of consciousness. Recurrently, for such periods as their work or study allows, they effect this through drugs or drunkenness or reckless sex, through motorised speed or disco dancing or mass raves or rock concerts; or, ubiquitously, by means of personal stereos or mobile phones plugging ears and removing minds. Or else, increasingly, as we have seen in Ireland during these last forty years, they opt for annihilating consciousness permanently; if female, often irresolutely and unsuccessfully, if male, usually with full resolution and success.

But it is mainly for mature consumers – for recurrent or habitual suspensions of their ordinary consciousness – that tons of mood-altering and hallucinatory drugs from Afghanistan, Columbia and other producer countries reach the West monthly. These serve, along with alcohol and self-immersion in mind-numbing work for weeks or months on end, when the consumers' acquired ability to ignore the pain proves insufficient. And there is one method of annihilating consciousness which is practised exclusively by mature adults, usually men. So regularly does it occur that we have recognised it as a malady characteristic of our times and given it the specific name, *rage*. 'Unmotivated' it is often termed, but wrongly so.

Senselessness thwarting reproduction

When senselessness is apprehended in the shared collective life, motivation to reproduce that life flags. In order to maintain population stability, a society's women must bear an average of about 2.1 children per lifetime. The fertility of white westerners now lies well beneath this. In the USA their rate is 1.8. According to the latest American government forecast, white people will be a minority there by 2042. The fertility rate for the European Union is 1.5 (for Ireland 1.85). In several of the larger European countries sharp declines in population are expected in the next twenty-five years.

The present demographic situation of the white West recalls two widely separated episodes. In the last phase of the western Roman Empire, when the rules of society were incoherently old-Roman and Christian – neither one nor the other integrally – the fertility and vigour of the Roman and romanised core declined. Only immigration, largely Germanic, kept the system functioning. Russia's utopian rule-changing in the first half of the last century differed from the later western experiment only in that it was Marxist-Leninist rather than left-liberal. In the latter decades of the Soviet Union before its collapse, Russians noted with dismay an increasing fall in their fertility rate, as opposed to that of the Union's Asian republics. In the foreseeable future they would be a minority in the Union.

But perhaps the most common instance of senselessness producing a collective will not to reproduce has been the so-called 'primitive tribe' in the American and other continents after a disruptive intrusion by Europeans had robbed its collective life of sense. (Significantly, among the ethnic groups in the USA, the only fertility rate lower than that of white people is the Native American or 'Red Indian'.) For any human community, small or large, it simply does not make sense to reproduce a collective life whose proffered framework for living fails to do that. In our case, however – that of the white race in the West – it is not a disruptive intrusion from outside that has presented us with a senseless framework. We have done that ourselves. So there is a protracted collective suicide in two acts: first, our presenting ourselves with an anti-human life, then our growing refusal to people it with more humans suffering the offence that we endure.

Consumerism's ersatz sense

Most of the time, most westerners manage to ignore the pain. On top of the training they have inherited from the generations before them in assessing for sense the life presented to them, another skin-deep training has been superimposed. From tender years onwards, the consumerist economy, and its accompanying teaching, condition them to accept an ersatz sense in place of the real sense they crave for.

This substitute sense has been provided, fundamentally, by the continuously increasing power to buy things and to do things, which the consumerist economy supplies to individual consumers as well as to states and business firms. The persuasive force of this increasing power to buy and do is actualised for the consumers in two interlocked ways. Repeatedly it enables them to acquire more, bigger or costlier things, and these things include the powers of new tools that enable them to do more things than they could previously. Among the many secondary powers thus conferred on consumers are the ability to pause a television programme while answering the phone, to use cellular phones for many things besides phoning, and to live lives increasingly longer than those of their ancestors.

While such benefits, in the eyes of most people, give material sense to the life on offer, a central message of the Correctorate's teaching furnishes it, for some people, with moral sense. This message, constantly repeated, tells us that those who think and live in accordance with the Correctorate's rules live a freer, more just and kinder life than the western generations that preceded them and than all the other peoples that have inhabited or that now inhabit the planet.

The net result is that most consumers, most of the time, believe in the surface of their minds that this present life of the western world is a good life. 'Stress', everyone recognises, stress of body and soul, regularly accompanies the living of this life. But stress with recurrent depression, most westerners resignedly accept, is an inevitable condition of living a life which despite all – despite even its moments of clear, shocking vision – is a good life.

That is the situation. And it is likely that, for as long as the buying and doing power of governments and consumers continues to increase, and the teaching that this contemporary western life is morally the best life ever known continues to have force for some, the West's senseless post-European system will continue to function. Dating its launch from that first, momentous rule change of 1945, it has still a few years to go before it matches the life span of its more conservatively post-western Soviet counterpart.

The life span of the American system is determined by the very transient nature of the two factors which, by supplying its ersatz sense, enable it to exist. Ultimately, for one reason or another, the continuous increase of the collective and individual power to buy and do – which provides both its main ersatz sense and its social glue – will cease. And its vaunted moral superiority over all previous or existing lives will become an irrelevant twaddle. Nothing will then remain to prevent direct and continuous impact of the system's senselessness on the consciousness of westerners, young and old, or to make that senseless and unloved life framework seem a good life. With no sense-making, respected set of rules to fall back on as a comforting matrix of order in the reduced material circumstances, the inevitable will happen. The chaos of the prevailing values and rules will be transformed into a violent social chaos without many precedents in history. All that idealism, that naïve and unanchored idealism, will go up in smoke!

In conclusion

The fact that this chaos looms as an inevitable outcome of the present condition of the West is the final light thrown on that condition by this recognition of the Second American Revolution and its context, and this tracing of its nature and outcome within the West. For historians the most valuable element of this exercise is likely to be the recognition of the revolution's context: the fact that it was one of three more or less simultaneous efforts by Europeans to found, in place of European civilisation, a rules system that would enable them to do more things and bigger things righteously, while eliminating inherited wrong practices and mindsets.

Those three efforts viewed together, each of them supported by millions of people, indicated a strong conviction among twentieth-century Europeans, in Europe and overseas, that the civilisation which their ancestors created, and which enabled them to dominate and lead the world, had ended its usefulness – had had its day. Clearly, by believing that, they made it a fact: a fact for historians of the twentieth century to record, if they are doing their job right.

The period since then, and continuing ahead of us beyond the collapse of the American liberal utopia, future historians will call 'transitional' and compare it to the transitional period between the civilisations of ancient Rome and Europe. Whether it will prove to be as long as that was or shorter, it will end in a new civilisation, or new civilisations, in the West. The plural is the more likely outcome: the United States, ever more involved with China and Japan, and domestically more Hispanic, is likely to pay little heed to Europe. Whether or how the new civilisation in Europe or in North America will be ethically more empowering than was Europe's is an open question. But that civilisation in one form or another will return in the West is certain, The ineradicable human craving for sense in life will ensure that.

*

The purpose of the above account of the present age in the West is to render the age we live in broadly intelligible. My readers will have noticed that this is best achieved by excluding moral judgment: by simply recounting What was done, by Whom, Why, *and* What, as a result, is now the case. *The constant application of moral characterisation and judgment is the fundamental cause of misrepresentation in the West's prevailing account of its history and nature since the 1930s. The main theme of the prevalent narrative is the proposition that the USA, Great Britain and their West European allies are 'good' by reason of the values and rules they uphold, their forms of government, and – in general if not in detail – the actions they engage in abroad. The principal subordinate theme, serving as reinforcement and corollary of that main theme, is that those nations and persons whom those 'good' powers have designated as enemies were or are 'evil'. The effort to maintain the validity of these theses through thick and thin makes the narrative necessarily capricious with regard to the facts of the matter. Obliged to use facts, silences, misrepresentations and fictions to support that dual proposition, it cannot be an account of the age which provides understanding of* What was done, by Whom, Why, *and* What, as a result, is now the case.

So powerful and pervasive in our age is the compulsion to moralise – read and listen to the mass media, including the health and safety ads! – that even those who offer alternatives to the prevalent moral tale of the age merely vary the tenor of the moralising. A new television documentary on Saddam Hussein promises to show us 'the man behind the monster' – thus retaining the fiction that Saddam was to a non-human degree a bad person. Or reversing the main proposition of the established moral tale, a Noam Chomsky or a John Pilger depicts America, Britain, the West generally, or Israel, as evil incarnate at work in the world.

It is only by noting this pervasive compulsion to moralise, and the accompanying demand that narrative take this form, that I can begin to understand why the three related historical facts on which my account of the age is based have been ignored by other writers. Those three entirely observable facts are the American rejection and experimental replacement of the accepted rules of western civilisation, the broad temporal coincidence of this with similar rejections and replacements in Russia and Germany, and the co-option of Western Europe into participation in the still continuing American experiment. From the perception and divulgation of those three perceptible facts, all real understanding of the present western age flows. Noting, therefore, the pervasive compulsion to moralise, I conclude that neither the purveyors of the prevalent view of the age, nor the conventionally 'radical' dissenters from it, could find in those obvious historical facts any grist for their moralising mills. Though central to the recent history and present condition of the West, those facts lay outside the set frameworks of their respective moralising schemes and were therefore ignored as simply not serviceable.

Ireland's Call

In a symposium published by the American magazine *Cineaste* in 1999, the Irish film-maker Bob Quinn said with reference to Ireland: 'Now that this country has finally shed its antediluvian religious beliefs, its national identity, its sense of personal and communal responsibility, its ethical inhibitions, its political sovereignty, even its own currency, all those things that retarded it for so long, the future glows with promise'. Clearly, the promise that Quinn saw was the Irish, stripped bare, becoming as much the founders of the civilisation that will follow Europe's as were the ancient Irish, through their monks and scholars, founders of European civilisation.

Faced with the situation brought about by the demolition of that civilisation on both sides of the Atlantic during the last sixty odd years, and the pressing need of westerners for an equivalent replacement, our comparative advantage is evident. Our abandonment of our high culture, native language and legal system centuries back gave us a head start. Our recent shedding of our remaining inheritances finished the job, made our clearing operation the most thorough. We are among western nations the most non-nation, the least distinguished by inherited features. We have produced a clean slate; a *tabula rasa* which by dint of being the most complete is also the most inviting and enabling. It is a situation crying out for new construction, led by the Irish, from San Francisco to Budapest.

A creative future offered to a people does not make itself. It is made by being seized and worked on by the social element of that people which has the particular capacity that the offered future requires; in this instance, Irishmen who, along with good will directed towards themselves, their fellow citizens and other westerners, have the ability to think critically and constructively, to imagine boldly, and to act accordingly. From our history since 1916 – that liberating heave we gave to the colonised world of Africa and Asia, more recently, our tigerish relocation of relative wealth and poverty within the European Union – we know that our country produces men with that ability.

Our eminently practical Industrial Development Authority knows it. Its latest poster advertising worldwide what Ireland offers the foreign investor shows the head of Bono, a globally thinking Irishman, and the words 'The Irish Mind'. That this collective mind of proven efficacy can be effectively directed to leading the re-civilisation of the West is obvious. Add the facility of cultural reconstruction which our cleanest of clean slates offers, and the luminous future for Ireland which Bob Quinn perceived passes out of the category of mirage into that of something that can realistically happen.

The fact is that the crying human need for a well-grounded, hierarchical and life-covering set of values and rules that makes sense will sooner or later compel work to meet this need. Sooner or later a post-European civilisation will take shape. Or more likely, two different civilisations will emerge in Europe and North America. Given that we cannot know how precisely it will turn out, let our focus be on Europe where we Irish have some experience, historically, in this kind of thing.

It is certain that in Europe the coming new civilisation – which might or might not again extend across the Atlantic – will be brought about by rejecters of the senseless mish-mash which now masquerades among us as a framework for life. As the core of the sense-providing framework which will replace it, Muslim rejecters will urge a westernised Islam; Christians, the Christian rules reformulated; and other formations of nay-sayers will promote sets of rules drawn from faiths and clusters of values for which we have as yet no names. In other words, there will be competing projects. But certain again is this much: that the rejecters who will generate and grow the new civilisation will do three things.

First, they will begin to present a hierarchy of values and rules, centred on a supreme, transcendental value, that satisfies, more profoundly than its rivals, the perennial human need for sense-in-life. That ordered assembly of values and rules, drawing on human experience and reason and on divine revelation, will be attentive to the specific needs, mindset and memories of contemporary Europeans. Along with the new elements which define it as a new civilisation, it will include values and rules extracted from the current mish-mash and from European civilisation.

Second, these canny and impassioned builders will win a growing acceptance of their new presentation of human life sensibly lived.

And finally – for a civilisation needs rulers – they, or more likely those to whom they transmit their impetus, will produce rulers or win the adherence of rulers. Rulers, that is, whose adherence is by way of service, and whose natural desire to manipulate the new sense-making scheme will be firmly resisted by its doctrinal protectors.

That is the enterprise which our Irish *tabula rasa* cleared of our past, and the proven efficacy of the Irish mind, fit us pre-eminently to set in motion, finding allies in the process. While, moreover, we are so engaged, that same liberation from our past will enable us, in an unsentimental backward look, to select from it, pragmatically, elements which can serve well again for Post-Europe.

But our first care must be to ensure that we are thinking and acting in the light of present reality; in real awareness of the present situation as it is. That entails close scrutiny, and perhaps correction, of the account of the present situation that I have given here. When that has been done, and we are as sure as we can be that we have a true grasp of how things are now in the West, our first tentative, constructive thinking can begin.

*

After I had added 'Ireland's Call' to the longer essay on my website, a few people asked me, 'Well, what shape do you think the post-European civilisation will have?' I answered that they were jumping the gun. I had thrown out the idea that Irish people with a mind for that sort of thing might tackle that question constructively. Starting with the picture of the age I had sketched, they might discuss with me whether I had got it more or less right. I did indeed get some feedback, touching on details rather than on the general picture. But at the same time, the clarity which that picture was throwing on particular matters that presented themselves from day to day encouraged me to feel that, whatever its defects might be, it was a useful tool. And the experience of finding that it was indeed such a tool distracted me from speculation about the future; glued me to the now. I felt compelled to offer to readers further insights into the present that I was deriving from the overall picture.

It struck me, too, that in time to come, after this present age has ended, a certain record of what it looked like and felt like, day to day, from inside – and specifically in Ireland and viewed from Ireland – might be both interesting in itself and a corrective supplement to what the official records of the age, including its leading newspapers, reported. Regard, then, what follows as extended footnotes to 'The Second American Revolution and the Sense Famine in the West'.

A Public Ritual Well Performed

12 May 2008

Yesterday I was in Tullamore and Clara, both in County Offaly, witnessing the preparations for the celebratory homecoming of Brian Cowen, the new Taoiseach. In each case, because I wanted to avoid the huge crowds, I left before he arrived, accompanied by his wife and children. Both in the county town where he lives, and in his native village, there was a great bustle of preparation and a joyous anticipation.

It was the final act in a ritual of transition from one taoiseach to the next which has given me great pleasure to observe. It was both a public ritual well performed and a public acceptance of its legitimacy as a handing over of political power. Over a month ago, on the steps of Government Buildings and surrounded by his Cabinet, the former taoiseach Bertie Ahern announced his intention to resign. A month-long 'lap of honour' followed, marked by public tributes to his performance as taoiseach and by various symbolic events. These included his address to the American Congress and concluded with his symbolic meeting on the Boyne with Northern Ireland's First Minister, Ian Paisley. They met there to open the Battle of the Boyne interpretative centre. In the meantime, Brian Cowen, the successor he had designated and who very aptly bore the Tánaiste title, was elected president-in-waiting of the main ruling party, Fianna Fáil.

Came the date preannounced by Ahern for his resignation and events succeeded each other rapidly: Ahern's visit to Áras an Uachtaráin to hand back his seal of office to the President; Cowen's confirmation by his party as its president; his election by the Dáil as Taoiseach; his visit in turn to Áras an Uachtaráin; his naming of his Cabinet, and the definitive seal on the new order of government secured by a second visit to the President. Finally, then, yesterday, like a Roman triumphator returning home, Cowen's festive return to his particular place in Ireland and his particular people there.

My pleasure in all of that has arisen partly from its being ritual well performed – a prescribed set of actions, carried out with punctiliousness and dignity, that bear meaning for a watching nation. But combined with that pleasure there was patriotic satisfaction: this was the Irish State displaying its existence and its legitimacy and having both reaffirmed by its citizens.

It was a consoling pleasure inasmuch as it made evident that at least that much of what the Irish Revolution intended survives healthily in form, if not in substance. Not that our state, as it is, is without practical as well as symbolic value: it played a vital role in the production of our recent and present wealth. But form it is rather than the substance which the Revolution intended for it. Since we adhered to the united-Europe enterprise, it is not a sovereign but a sort of Home Rule state. Neither is it, as the Revolution intended it would be, the state of a nation that is intellectually self-determining and culturally self-shaping; that is to say. a normal nation. That had not existed in Ireland since the destruction and dissolution of the Gaelic nation: but the Revolution explicitly intended we should become that, as the song says, 'once again'. More precisely, it wanted us to become that in the conventional contemporary shape: as a sovereign nation-state such as was the norm in Europe up to the Second World War; a sort of Denmark, say, as Denmark was before the united-Europe enterprise.

We managed, though still emigrating in large numbers, to be something like that, politically, after Britain surrendered the Treaty ports and during the World War years. But we had not, by then, yet managed to be a Denmark intellectually or culturally. Nor, more fundamentally, had we by then achieved what the Revolution assumed would follow from political sovereignty: a self-sustaining economy that would end the pathological emigration, thus enabling the nation, as the basis for all else,to remain substantially at home. And our failure to achieve that by the 1950s proved fatal to the entire revolutionary programme.

We had not achieved it owing to the persistence after Independence of the self-doubt planted in our deeply colonised souls. That blocked the emergence of a sufficiency of native economic enterprise. such as had produced in Norway, after its independence from Sweden in 1905, an economic upsurge meeting the nation's needs. Even if by the 1950s we had been prosperous, we would still have needed great luck to become intellectually and culturally a normal nation. We would have needed great luck because of our small population, our ingrained self-doubt, our meagre inherited culture, and our location. We were a liberal-democratic, English-speaking entity situated between the two largest English-speaking nations, at a time when technology was greatly increasing their ability to communicate beyond their borders.[1] But being at that juncture, the 1950s, not prosperous – on the contrary in dire straits economically and demographically – put paid to any chance of intellectual autonomy or a culture shaped by ourselves.

It put paid to it because it drove us, from the late 1950s onwards, to make the acquisition of material sufficiency for the nation *in any form and by any means* our ruling passion; something to be attained at any cost. And in the western world, as it was then in the process of constituting itself, a West European nation, situated and circumstanced as we were, could acquire material sufficiency only at a very high cost. The price was so high because the two available suppliers of material sufficiency to the Republic of Ireland had the ability to set a high price and did so. One of them, the supplier to the west of us, the United States of America, had in the wake of the war established imperial supremacy over Western Europe. In return for its favour, protection and productive investment, it required that its European satellites adopt its ideological answer to Communism and recipe for great wealth; namely, its post-European, post-Christian worldview, complete with a collection of rules-to-live-by known as consumerist liberalism. The other supplier, to the east of us, the united-Europe enterprise, required, as the price for the massive subsidies it was willing to pay us, that the Republic surrender its nation-state sovereignty to a higher authority in Brussels, in which it would participate in accordance with its relatively minor weight. Our sovereign state, given its now ruling passion for material sufficiency in any form and by *any means*, had no realistic option to refuse those high prices and it paid both of them.

Fair play to it, even decapitated, as it were, and shorn of the possibility of being the state, let alone the sovereign state, of an intellectually self-determining and culturally self-shaping nation, it bargained and wheedled well in Europe and administered well at home. We emerged with much more than material sufficiency for the Republic's citizens, now functioning as globalised consumers. We have had ten years of huge growth rates, a higher per capita GDP than Britain, material sufficiency for tens of thousands of immigrants, and the envy of every small country in Europe and elsewhere that has not yet 'made it'.

---

[1] This ability, exercised by the USA, was to result by the early 2000s in our urban Irish people writing and speaking American English with Irish accents, and sometimes, to show they were really 'hip', also using American spellings.

I was deeply attached to the aims of the Irish Revolution. In sympathy with it, I wanted Ireland to become a normal European nation-state, such as Denmark or the Netherlands or Sweden or Hungary – to mention only some of the smaller ones – were within living memory. So I have been pained to see that not happening. That is why my pleasure, these last weeks, in witnessing the Irish state's well-executed passage of leadership, had a consoling quality. Full consolation it was not by any means, but it was some.

Thug rud eile pléisiúr mór dom sna laetha seo. Nuair a rinne Brian Cowen a chéad óráid sa Dáil mar an Taoiseach nua, labhair sé ar dtús ar feadh fiche neomat nó mar sin i nGaeilge líofa. Niorbh é an gnáth 'chúpla focal' ach cuid substaintiúil den óráid nár athdhúirt se nuair a lean sé leis as Béarla. Ar ócáid phoibli eile i rith na seachtaine labhair sé Gaeilge arís ar feadh píosa. Tá sé ag tabhairt le fios, sílim, go mbeidh labhairt na Gaeilge mar chuid dá stíl. [2]

---

[2] Transl. Something else gave me pleasure in these days. When Brian Cowen made his first speech in the Dáil as new Taoiseach, he began by speaking for twenty minutes or so in fluent Irish. It wasn't the usual cúpla focal but a substantive part of the speech, which he did not repeat when he continued in English. On another public occasion during the week he again spoke Irish for some time. I think he is signalling that speaking Irish will be part of his style.

Totalitarianism Domesticated

Wednesday 14 May
This morning after five o'clock I was out walking with about fifty others in the leafy grounds of Maynooth College. We were there to listen to the birds' 'dawn chorus'. I recalled that the last time I had done this was in the 1970s with eight Russians, near the datcha owned by one of them in the outskirts of Moscow. The day before, in the city, I had been to the square where stamp collectors met once a week to exchange and trade postage stamps. And it occurred to me, not for the first time, between the trilling of a blackbird and the hooting of a wood pigeon, that 'totalitarianism' has had an unjustly bad press in the West.

Because the Soviet Union of the Cold War years was the enemy of the West, our politicians and mass media encouraged us to believe that life there was like life in Orwell's fictional Nineteen-Eighty-Four. Big Brother, or rather, his collective, police equivalent, was spying on every action, penetrating every thought. Cowed citizens, their lives minutely regulated, moved in serried ranks through dreary working days. The point was to have us believe that life in the 'totalitarian' Soviet Union, from the 1950s to the 1980s – when it had become a post-revolutionary, settled society – was the polar opposite of that bright and free life that the West called 'democracy', and hence a bad and hateful life, worth fighting against.

However, as I remarked in an essay on 'Myth and Reality of the Twentieth Century' in my last book, in the latter part of the twentieth century that western caricaturing decreased. More and more westerners visited the Soviet Union, and some of them noticed features redolent of the Soviet model present or emerging in their own societies, especially in the USA. Since the attack on the Twin Towers, and security measures which were once considered totalitarian have become, in much more efficient forms, part of western life, westerners have further revised their view of their own societies. Two things which have long been the case have become apparent to many of them: we live in a western-style totalitarian system, and its totalitarian features, while occasionally exasperating, are tolerable and in some respects comforting, if kept within bounds.

What set me thinking again about this, before this morning in the woods revived the thought, was the blurb of a new British book I saw advertised a few days ago online. The book is called *Surveillance Unlimited*, the author Keith Laidler. That online blurb seemed to encapsulate how what had once seemed horrors to be found only in *Nineteen Eighty Four* and Communist countries are coming to be accepted – Big Brother even gets a mention! – as part of the British everyday. Always, of course, with the proviso that they are 'kept within bounds'. Watch how the tendency of the following text changes half-way through:

> "Your car is satellite-tracked, your features auto-identified on video, your e-mails, faxes and phone calls monitored. You are covertly followed via transmitters implanted in your clothes, via your switched-off mobile and your credit-card transactions. Your character, needs and interests are profiled by surveillance of every website you visit, every newsgroup you scan, every purchase you make. Big Brother is here, quietly adding to your files in the name of government efficiency and the fight against organised crime and terrorism.
>
> As the author argues in this urgent, important book, the potential for abuse is far-reaching and formidable. *Surveillance can indeed fight crime. But at what price? Is the deployment of such technologies even legal? What will be their effects on the fabric of society? And what can we do to prevent the worst excesses?* This book has the answers." *(Italics mine.)*

A totalitarian system is of course about more than surveillance. It was in the 1970s that I noticed its first signs in Ireland as the three main Dublin newspapers gradually lost their plurality of viewpoint and worldview. They were conforming to the consumerist-liberal line that had been pioneered in the 60s by *The Irish Times* and RTÉ. People began referring to 'the media' as to a single voice. I recognised that in this respect Dublin had become like Communist Prague or Bucharest, while at the same time we were hearing daily that over there were Oppression and Indoctrination in contrast to the Freedom and Free Expression that existed here. It was then that my visits to the Soviet Union and Communist Eastern Europe began to help me recognise the western similarities.

Let's clarify what totalitarianism is; let's attempt a definition and then, if necessary, correct or add to it. A notable benefit of such clarification will be to realise that the confrontation of the Cold War was not, as we were taught, between two essentially different political systems embodying Evil and Good, but between two essentially similar political systems which constituted the grey everyday of the twentieth century.

Adapting a working definition I used in a footnote in my introductory essay, a totalitarian state is 'a state which involves itself authoritatively, in tandem with a secular teaching authority, in all aspects of the citizens' lives'. So the entity in question is not simply a state. It is a state and a secular teaching authority involving themselves, collaboratively and authoritatively, in all aspects of the citizens' lives'. What to call that hybrid entity – since no name for it has emerged to match its adjective? A *totalitarium* will do; it has the requisite all-enveloping sound. To describe our western-style, democratic version, the term 'soft totalitarianism' has emerged. Claudio Magris, in whose writings I first came across it, defines it as a system 'capable of inducing the masses to believe that they want what their rulers consider appropriate'. As to the respective effectiveness of the two kinds, it seems likely that our western kind, by using 'softer' methods, wins.

Broadly speaking, it is a form of rule that goes back to Babylon and ancient Egypt. Broadly speaking, because then the state-endorsed teaching authority was religious rather than secular, and both it and the state lacked the technology for affecting the masses that we have today. Again in broad terms, it reappeared in Europe in the absolute monarchies of the seventeenth and eighteenth centuries, regimes marked by the rule of the 'union of Throne and Altar'.

Nothing new under the sun, as they say, though we have been taught to believe that everything about this age of ours, since, say, the First World War, is as radically new as the New World supposedly brought into being by the First American Revolution or by the French Jacobins' declaration of Year One. The point of such teaching is, by disconnecting mass consciousness from historical precedents, to make it more receptive for scary fairy tales about present enemies, and generally more easily manipulable. Dictatorship? A demoniacal invention by Fascists, Communists and other assorted Bad Men in the twentieth century. In reality, no. In reality, and for the umpteenth time since ancient Egypt, sole rule by an unelected man who has the decisive say in the group of co-rulers who enable him to rule.

In the Republic the Data Protection Commissioner has the job of 'keeping within bounds' the invasion of privacy by means of surveillance or otherwise. Mr Hawkes' annual report, which came out a few days ago, recorded a threefold increase in a two-year period in the number of complaints received. Reading again the newspaper report, I realise that my working definition of a totalitarium does not cover the precise nature of our Ameropean version because it does not make explicit the role of business. A considerable number of the cases which Mr Hawkes investigated had to do with invasions of privacy by commercial enterprises. Most of these took the form of intrusive marketing in the form of unsolicited text messages to mobile phones. But there was also a hotel which used a covert CCTV camera to monitor transactions in the bar, and a health club which had cameras in the private areas of a sauna and steam room. (I gather that twelve American airports have installed a security scanner which shows passengers minus their clothes!)

In the 'Second American Revolution' essay I pointed out that our 'teaching authority', the liberal Correctorate, operating mainly through the media, is a hybrid of liberal ideologues and business people telling us how to act, speak, think and be. But the active role of business in our totalitarium goes beyond the delivery of its teaching through mass-media advertising. It pressurises and blackmails governments, it intrudes in citizens' lives in the ways Mr Hawkes mentions. In defining, not all totalitariums but our consumerist-liberal kind, that would need to be explicitly indicated. Perhaps simply by saying 'a state, a secular teaching authority, and business, involving themselves, collaboratively and forcefully, in all aspects of the citizens' lives'.

Actually here I find myself wrestling with precisely the problem that de Tocqueville encountered in 1840 when he was prophesying the kind of power that would in the end rule the liberal democracies: the problem, namely, of finding a word or words to describe it. De Tocqueville did not entertain, even in passing, that it might be a parliament, or a government indirectly elected, or both of those combined with a judiciary. He said merely that this ultimate ruling power would be both absolute and of an entirely new kind. A 'tyranny' would not describe it nor would any of the words with similar meaning that had traditionally been used. When it came to opting for a word or words, he side-stepped in this manner:

> "The first thing that strikes the observation is an innumerable multitude of men all equal and alike, incessantly trying to procure the petty and paltry pleasures with which they glut their lives. Above this race of men there stands an immense and tutelary power… That power is absolute, minute, regular, provident and mild. It would be like the

authority of a parent, if, like that authority, its object was to prepare men for manhood; but it seeks on the contrary to keep them in perpetual childhood. It is well content that the people should have a good time, provided they think of nothing but having a good time...."

And so on, as I have quoted elsewhere. Perhaps, then, I should be content with saying that the contemporary West is ruled by 'a Power which is immense, tutelary, absolute, minute, regular, provident and mild', and into the bargain 'hybrid'; and leave it at that. But it is not true that a single Power with those qualities rules the entire West. Rules the USA yes: that great nation is its own self-contained, self-ruling totalitarium. But in the totalitarium that is Europe today, it is a matter of a ruling Power made up of intermeshed ruling powers.

Keeping in mind that each of the powers that rules Europe is itself hybrid, there is the USA to some degree; in great part there is Brussels; and to a diminishing degree the residual nation-states of Europe rule. Exercising power of the nod-and-wink kind, America persuaded the Irish government to permit the use of Shannon airport as a military transit base in its war against and in Iraq. It derived its leverage from the fact that American firms have been playing a big role in the Irish prosperity of recent years, and that the Irish government would like that situation to continue. As to Brussels, only about a third of new law-making in the Republic is done by our elected parliament, the rest by the Commission of the European Union, seated in Brussels.

If certain Irish farmers can no longer cut turf on a certain nearby bog or graze sheep on a particular mountain; or if a label stating the name of the breeder must appear on every chop in a butcher's shop; or Irish fishermen must throw into the sea fish which they have caught in excess of their quota; or a man must take care to avoid punishment when writing or speaking publicly about persons who are not straight white males – that is because Brussels has decreed it. There is also a roundabout way for Brussels to command. If a pub owner in a Mayo village may no longer smoke his pipe in his own pub or allow his customers to smoke with their drinks, that is because a minister of the Irish government was given the power by Brussels to ordain so by decree, bypassing our parliament; and used that delegated power.

The Commission in Brussels has the sole power to make legislative proposals valid for the Union as a whole. Business lobbyists contribute to these by inspiring or helping to shape them. The Council of Ministers, composed of the heads of government of the member states, meets regularly to approve, reject or modify the proposed directives which the Commission submits to it. It would not, then, be surprising to find that these heads of government instigate the Commission to propose Union laws which it would be difficult or impossible to get through their own parliaments; an obvious example being the ban on smoking in pubs and other places of social resort. (As it happens, on 12 June there is to be a referendum on a proposed remodelling of the European Union, the so-called Lisbon Treaty, and two campaigns are in progress, for a Yes and a No. I will come back to this.)

In sum, and leaving aside America's veiled participations in the governance of the Irish Republic, *most* laws and regulations which descend on us, requiring obedience, do so as if from heaven, without there being anyone known to us whom we can hold responsible. The democratic ritual which allows us every few years to elect a governing group for the Irish Republic from an ideologically homogenised political class does not alter this state of affairs. Our situation, in that respect, is formally no different from that of the other members of the European Union. But the much larger populations of some of them give their governments a more effective role than ours in the determination of the Brussels laws and regulations that descend on us as if from heaven. The Republic's weight in the 27-member Union ranks somewhat less than that of Lithuania, say, in the old 15-member Soviet Union.

This, essentially, is the framework of command within which the left-liberal Correctorate and international business play their respective parts in shaping our lives. In Brussels, the resident corrrectorate ensures that commands issuing from there conform to liberal doctrine or at least do not contravene it. In the member-states, the national correctorates execute three tasks. They see to it that those Brussels directives which serve liberal purposes are added effectively to the consumers' rules to live by; they vet national legislation for its liberal orthodoxy; and through the local mass media and fellow-travelling institutions they maintain regular instruction of politicians and people in correct behaviour, thought, judgment and language, and vehemently condemn deviance. Business, through its advertising campaigns, contributes to this pedagogy, while exciting desire for things and physical persons. More concretely, it determines prices, gives or withdraws remunerative employment, and works at

39

persuading Brussels and the national governments to facilitate its operations.

It seems, then, that to accommodate our Ameropean totalitarium, a final adjustment to the definition tried above is needed. Our totalitarium is 'a composite political structure (instead of 'a state'), a secular teaching authority, and international business, involving themselves, collaboratively and forcefully, in all aspects of the consumers' lives'.

Like the vast majority of people since history began, the vast majority of people from eastern Poland to western Ireland are normally little concerned about where the laws and regulations come from, or the structure of the power that rules their lives. What matters to them is the kind of life it delivers. Because – except in one respect, and that not a material one – the hybrid Power that rules them delivers, as lives go, a pretty good life, normally they ignore it and get on with living. That occasionally it delivers annoyances, goes without saying; but they cope with these as they cope with bad weather. While they participate in the traditional, exciting, 'democratic' rituals that purport to give them power over their lives, the notion of actually exercising such power would seem to all but a few of them a distraction from living. More power than they have, they do want, very naturally; but this desire is being constantly satisfied by their continually increasing power to buy, and the ability this gives them to purchase, or pay for the use of, empowering devices of all kinds from mobile phones to aeroplanes. Western rulers have found in our time that the provision of this kind of increasing power makes unnecessary the real or pretended concession of increasing political power which their predecessors made to their subjects.

Now, however, with this referendum on the Lisbon Treaty to be held in Ireland, and nowhere else, things are in this rare instance somewhat different. The Irish in the Republic are being asked to decide by their votes – there are various issues, but this seems the core issue – whether they want Brussels to have greater power over them than hitherto, and the Irish Republic to have even less than the little it has. They are being asked to make a decision about a matter which most of them never think about: the structure of the principal power that rules their lives. And, judging by the campaigning that has started to get under way, a considerable number seems to believe that this matters to them.

The New Arrivals among the Statues

Thursday 15 May
During my years in Italy, Dublin's O'Connell Street was redesigned. That much I noticed on a visit home a few years ago. The footpaths on both sides had been greatly widened, a broad walkway with new trees laid out in the centre, the spaces for the passage of motor traffic greatly reduced. In 2003 the 'Spire' was erected at the central point of the street's length. It occupied the spot where Nelson's Pillar, honouring the famous British admiral, had stood for 158 years until it was blown up by the IRA in the late 1960s.

For years there had been debate about what should replace it. Because the spot was not only at the centre of Ireland's capital but also adjacent to the GPO which had played a central role in the 1916 Rising, there was an assumption that the replacement should have a national symbolic significance. A statue of Pearse or Connolly, or of both, or a monument in some way honouring Ireland's freedom struggle, were the most frequent suggestions put forward and talked about. Then in 2002 the city council sponsored an international competition and chose 'The Spire'. It is a tapering spike of glistening steel, 390 feet tall, designed by Ritchie Architects of London. When I first saw it, I remarked that it would have been more suitable for the other Blackpool,* the popular English seaside resort, than for the centre of Ireland's capital city. But on reflection, I recognised that it was at least an honest statement of the Republic's state of mind after its prudent self-effacement during the Northern War and during the past-effacing enrichment of the Celtic Tiger boom. It stood for, represented, and said Nothing. In this respect it expressed the newly ascendant public orthodoxy which the Australian writer William Buckley had noted in his book *Memory Ireland* in 1985 and sketched as follows:

> "Ireland is not a nation, once again or ever, so the new story runs, but two nations; maybe several; it does not have its characteristic religion – or, if it does, it ought not; it does not have its characteristic language, as anyone can see or hear; it has no particular race or ethnic integrity. Ireland is nothing – a no-thing – an interesting nothing, to be sure, composed of colourful parts, a nothing mosaic. It is advertising prose and Musak."

---

* Dublin, Dubhlinn, means 'black pool'.

Those changes notwithstanding, the basic iconography of the street remains intact. Roughly at the centre of the west side stands the pillared GPO with the Tricolour flying above it. Forming a triangle with the GPO, the monument to O'Connell the Liberator stands in the street at the south end, Parnell's monument at the other end. Beneath the pillared portico of the GPO, behind a large glass rectangle at the centre of the façade, stands the bronze statue of the skirted warrior Cúchulainn. To hold himself erect in spite of his wounds he has bound himself to the stump of a tree. Spear in hand, he is leaning to his left, his head drooped. A crow perched on his shoulder indicates that he has died and need no longer be feared by his enemies. On a slab beneath the statue, there is a quotation from the Easter Week Proclamation. It runs from 'We declare the right of the people of Ireland to the ownership of Ireland, and to the unfettered control of Irish destinies, to be sovereign and indefeasible,' down to the seven signatories underneath. Reading them, one inevitably recalls Yeats' line about 'spelling them out in a verse'. On the Liberator's monument 'O'CONNELL' suffices. A more or less permanent pigeon on his head besmirches more or less permanently his face. The tall granite pillar behind Parnell presents a golden harp and these words:

> "No man has a right to fix the boundary to the march of a nation. No man has a right to say to his country thus far shalt thou go and no further. We have never attempted to fix the ne-plus-ultra to the progress of Ireland's nationhood and we never shall."

Yesterday, walking along the street, it occurred to me that there is no statue of any twentieth-century figure apart from the labour leader, Jim Larkin who died in 1947. Not to mention the 1916 leaders, no de Valera, Collins, Douglas Hyde, Yeats or Lemass. After Larkin, the impulse to honour here by a statue or otherwise broke down.

As I was so thinking, I noticed something surprising on the street's central walkway, about a hundred paces north of The Spire. On a concrete plinth, behind a framed rectangle of glass, there was a lit-up human figure in walking motion. It was a slender figure, natural height, which for the lack of any evidence to the contrary seemed to represent a young man. The torso was composed of dots of yellow light; the head was a detached, featureless circle of light, bobbing in rhythm with its owner's walk. There were no feet. I guessed that, technically speaking, it was a LED or Light Emitting Diode. Closer inspection from where I was standing showed me that the entire rectangle was filled by regular rows of white dots. Those dots which were needed to represent the figure in motion became illuminated, or ceased to be lit up, as required. The figure was represented as dressed in a T-shirt and short pants; it had bare legs and short socks. Its walking motion was easy, lithe, suggesting general physical fitness and not a care in the world.

I crossed to the tree-lined central walkway. On the plinth beneath the framed rectangle I read 'Julian Opie: Julian walking 2007'. Then, lower again: 'Julian Opie: Walking on O'Connell St.' Mr Opie, I took it, was the maker of 'Julian walking'.

Spurred to further inspection of what the city fathers have been up to, I look beyond Father Mathew The Apostle of Temperance, in monk's robes, arms outstretched, towards the Parnell monument. And I see not far from Father Mathew what looks like another concrete plinth with superimposed framed glass rectangle And sure enough, approaching it, I see what looks like a brother or sister of 'Julian walking'. A slight protrusion of bum along with a discreet protrusion on chest – nothing mumsy, these are free-as-the-air unattached singles – decides for 'sister'. Moreover, the writing underneath says 'Julian Opie: Sara walking 2007'. Gender balance naturally, how could I think otherwise! Sara has the same detached bobbing circle for a head, She is wearing a sleeveless top and slacks. Two pegs protruding from the slacks serve as feet. Slender as Julian, she, too, has that easy, swinging walk. The word 'lithe' springs again to mind.

Perhaps, I thought, unknown to me O'Connell Street has become populated by such figures. Setting out to inspect, I turn back towards 'Julian walking' and The Spire, pass the latter, and sure enough, there is another of them, opposite the Cúchulainn window of the GPO. It is 'Jack walking'. What seems to be a scarf bobs in front of his neck; his upper garment is shorter than Julian's – is it actually shorter or simply tucked into his trousers? It covers his arms. His head, once again, is a separated, bobbing circle. Glancing at the Cúchulainn window, I see that Jack's reflection is superimposed on Cúchulainn. His illuminated upper body rises above the almost horizontal line formed by the flat top of the tree stump and the dead warrior's drooping upper body and neck descending to head.

About sixty paces further towards Jim Larkin, gender balance again maintained, 'Suzanne walking 2007'. Skirted this time, her skirt swinging as she walks. Arms bare, the merest suggestion of breast. Was her walk somewhat slower? It was hard to know as you moved from one of them to another, mesmerised.

I progressed to Jim Larkin, who still stood there high, his arms outstretched with hands upraised. His call, too, was still there: 'The great appear great because we are on our knees. Let us rise'. On the sides of his plinth, two quotations, from Patrick Kavanagh and Sean O'Casey respectively, still celebrated his greatness. The view onward to O'Connell, past Sir John Gray and William Smith O'Brien, was clear of innovation.

How, I asked myself, as I went off about my business, was I to understand the new arrivals? That in line with The Spire's non-utterance of anything, they were intended to say nothing, struck me first. But then, the placing of Jack in such a spot as to cancel, by his reflection in the GPO window, the statue of Cúchulainn, was that deliberate or merely accidental? Was it, or was it not, meant to 'say' something? I could not decide.

Clearly, taking The Spire and the LEDs together, the city fathers had decided that O'Connell Street would no longer be used to honour dead Irishmen (or indeed Irishwomen) who had served their compatriots well, or at least tried to do so. Notable objects would indeed be erected in line with the line of commemorative statues, but objects that, on the face of it, honoured nobody and said Nothing. About the reason for that, I could only guess. Was it that the city fathers believed that it was in general not a good thing to honour with monuments the meritorious dead, or merely that it was not good for Dublin in particular, or Ireland in general, to do this? Or perhaps not good to do any more of it; that we had done enough of that? Without going and asking them, I could not know.

But if Sara, Julian, Jack and Suzanne said nothing and commemorated no one, what did they *represent*? All portrayals of human figures, since the most ancient cave drawings of hunters and gatherers, have represented something; to begin with, human beings. Most obviously, these four human figures, in walking motion, represented young contemporary men and women. And by all appearances they were of the contemporary *genus* Singles. They did not in other words represent contemporary human beings as such, but the kind known as Singles. And there were further delimiting elements: they were slim, to all appearances healthy, and were wont to take exercise, either by doing what they were doing – walking – or otherwise, perhaps in gyms. They were also – an aspect, I suppose. of their 'contemporary' look – as near to unisex as representation of male and female could make them.

I said above, of one of them, 'without a care in the world', and it was true of all of them; they appeared so, and indeed it was part of what made them Singles. Did those detached, featureless, bobbing circles which represented their heads mean thoughtless as well as without care? It did seem so. And a final thing about them struck me: while not ugly, neither were they beautiful. Regardless of the artist's intention, the technique of representation he had used made that impossible. So it was excluded that, in the manner of some ancient Greek statues, they represented youthful physical beauty.

But it struck me, at the same time, that they represented ideal human beings; ideal, I mean, in terms of contemporary western canons of human excellence. And if, behind placing them there among those statues of Irishmen who had served Ireland by contributing to its freedom struggle (or in Cúchulainn's case by inspiring it), there was an illustrative intention, a minimal saying of Something, then it might lie in *just that*. 'All those leaders and heroes worked and struggled so that Irish men and women might be as these are: healthy, slender, unisex, well-exercised Singles without a care or a thought in the world.'

JOHN WATERS GETS IT ALMOST RIGHT

Friday 16 May

John Waters' column in *The Irish Times* today is headed 'Gay father case exposes media in thrall to victimology'. He is writing about 'the immense media interest', some time back, in the judgment given in a certain court case. A homosexual man was seeking custody and access rights in respect of his child which, with his consent, was living with a lesbian couple. The child had been born following a 'sperm donor' agreement between him and the couple. The man's application was denied. And then last week, when costs were awarded against him, the media showed no interest at all. John continues:

> "This provides further proof, if such were required, that the media nowadays are interested in neither facts nor justice – all that matters is the promotion of fashionable causes. This case was 'newsworthy' because it advanced the objective of lesbian parenting.
>
> The profound implications for father and child – not to mention society in general – were glossed over. This case illustrates rather better than usual that we no longer have news organisations, but machines of social agitation driven by a neurotic and aggressive ideology employing certain social issues as battering rams to demolish existing norms and install extremist solutions at the centre of reality.
>
> Normally, in pursuing its agendas, the media affects a concern for the marginalised, the dispossessed and the rejected, suggesting its interest in gay rights, for example, is motivated by a desire for a more 'tolerant' and 'compassionate' society. But the man in this case is gay and yet cannot call on the support or interest of the media.
>
> Why? Because all this talk about tolerance is just talk. What is useful about the gay issue is that it makes an excellent battering ram. Individual gay people are of no consequence. All that matters is the furtherance of the demolition agenda.
>
> Since costs in this case will likely exceed €400,000, last week's decision will probably result in this man being bankrupted, losing his home and having to begin again in middle age, cast out of the life of his son unless the triumphant lesbian couple decide otherwise. Consider this in the light of the oft-repeated assertions by figures of authority and influence that fathers must face their responsibilities. Here was a father who faced his responsibilities with courage and determination, and as a result faces financial ruin.
>
> Of course, such rhetoric is not to be taken literally, but as evidence of the dysfunction of a society which has ceased to perceive things in the

light of justice but understands only victimologies arising from the ideology of demolition.

Our central ethical system hinges not on right, or good, but on the inverted meritocracy created by the ideology. This pursues its logic by means of an unacknowledged points system, in which PC ratings are extended to categories of designated victim. Thus, the ideology can be identified in terms of iron laws of omnipotent victimhood.

Victims in this context are defined not so much by their objective circumstances as by the identity of their alleged 'oppressor'. Any kind of female victim trumps any kind of male. Females can only become oppressors if their victims are lower down the chain. A black lesbian disabled Traveller would have an almost 100 per cent victim rating. A straight, white, middle-class male close to a zero rating. And so forth. The man in this case may be gay – normally a strong card – but his gayness is a weak trump against the all-powerful claim of two lesbians seeking to force through a new norm....

Because politicians run scared of any reforms which might risk the disfavour of the ideology, politics has become socially irrelevant, and social change is mainly brought about not by those employed for this purpose but by judges acting in cases taken by individual citizens at enormous risk to themselves....

If the High Court judgment stands, in my view all unmarried fathers must accept that their entitlement to a relationship with their children is to be set at zero and that henceforth any such relationships will exist purely on a provisional basis, by the grace and favour of mothers....'

What John is doing here is using a particular case to throw some light on the reigning ideology in the Republic and how its application affects the lives of certain kinds of people. He is doing this in what is the principal print organ of the ideology endorsed by state and business, and therefore the main print organ of the Irish Correctorate. Doctrinally speaking, what *Pravda* was for Russian Communists, or what *The Catholic Standard* was in the Ireland of fifty years ago, *The Irish Times* is in the Republic today. It has employed John Waters as a weekly columnist for years; and even when in recent years he has become increasingly a strong critic of its doctrines, it has retained him. It does so because it is liberal practice to afford dissidents and ideological critics a marginal public space. Partly this is done for the purpose – in the case of John it often works – of making the liberal faithful grateful to the Correctors for keeping that space marginal.

John's account of this ideological situation and of some of its workings is the fullest account I have read in any Irish newspaper. Given the limitations imposed by its setting, it is remarkable. Necessarily, however, and perhaps in part because John's view of the reality is incomplete, it falls somewhat short of the full picture.

When, in the context of the case he is discussing, John writes of 'the media', he is being inexact. He does not in fact mean the Irish mass media of all kinds from Donegal via Dublin to Wexford and Kerry. There is frequently a loose usage of 'the media' to refer to *The Irish Times* and RTÉ, the semi-state broadcaster, which since it was established in the 1960s has followed, ideologically, the lead of the *Times*. Perhaps this is the case here with John's usage. But whether it is or not, what he in fact means is 'the liberal mass media', in the sense of those elements of the mass media which – while none dissents from it – notably make a point of following the left-liberal line. Such 'elements' can range from one or more daily newspapers and monthly magazines to a single well-known contributor to a local broadcasting station. Ultimately what John is referring to, and what for exactitude he would need to indicate with his own choice of word, is what I term the Correctorate: namely, that informally cohering group of idealists of liberal conviction which, mainly through various media organs, as employees or outside contributors, teaches, exhorts and reproves the nation, and zealously tries to guide it.

Such precise identification would again be useful when John speaks of 'the media' confining themselves today to promoting 'fashionable causes'. He is not referring to causes that are actually 'fashionable', in the sense of favoured by the chattering classes and fashionable society – quite on the contrary. The causes in question are causes which the Correctorate deems important for its purposes and has been able to impose as topics on the mass media, regardless of whether they are of general interest or not.

Then again, when John attributes predominant agency to a 'neurotic and aggressive ideology' he misses the reality. An ideology cannot be an agency: the agency he has in mind is that aforementioned party of teaching ideologues. When he writes that 'politicians run scared of any reforms which might risk the disfavour of the ideology', he means that they run scared of the disfavour of the Correctorate; as years ago many of them took good care not to displease the previous state-endorsed teaching authority, the Catholic Church. That the Correctorate, though often 'neurotic and aggressive', has, besides demolition, also construction in mind; John concedes early on when he writes of it working 'to demolish existing norms *and install extremist solutions*' *(italics mine.)*. But later he seems to give what he terms its 'demolition agenda' undue emphasis. In fairness to the Correctorate.

its purpose and work is not to create an ethical vacuum, but to replace the old rules with new, morally superior rules.

John himself cites some of these when, having mentioned the new 'omnipotent' value given to victimhood, he spells out the new 'iron laws' derived from it. The Correctorate is trying, by experimenting with a collection of rules-for-living that have never before been tried, to bring about, in ethical and physical terms, a perfect human condition. (Or rather, a condition imperfect only in that death, while it is for most people being continuously postponed, is not abolished.)

'Our central ethical system', writes John, 'hinges not on right, or good, but on the inverted meritocracy created by the ideology'. He is referring to the ethical system taught by the Correctorate and to the meritocracy of victimhood which this has established. But because this is indeed an ethical system, it is not strictly true that it does not hinge on right or good. It hinges on concepts of right and good which differ from those of the old European civilisation, and consequently, because John still adheres to these, from his own. For the liberals, recognition of the intrinsic equality of persons by according them equal rights and treatment is a very great ethical good.

In European civilisation various categories of person did not have their equality thus recognised. Left-liberals aim to compensate those traditionally oppressed or victim categories by privileging them on a scale corresponding to the degree of their previous victimisation. Liberal investigation of that victimisation has determined that this confers on Travellers, the disabled, homosexuals and women, an ascending degree of merit, and consequently of right to compensatory privilege. In the case in question – a matter of recognising the common human right of everyone to parenting – a fine reckoning gives two homosexual females precedence over one homosexual man.

It is true that, in the moral reckoning of liberals – who are predominantly male – men as such come out badly, and white, heterosexual, able, middle-class, settled men rate less than zero. But given that in the old order, all those kinds of men were to a greater or lesser degree privileged categories, that is for liberals only just. Fathers, clergy, parents, teachers and the aged also enjoyed, simply by being that, privilege and authority of varying degree. They, too, must in justice purge that inequality for the common good. For liberals all this compensatory rearrangement is simply a matter of operating as Divine Justice will operate on the Day of Judgment.

Some, in accordance with their merits or demerits in the previous life, must up, and some must down.

I am now talking playfully, but what else but grim hilarity is called for when considering the senselessness of a rules system which, imposed on the white race in the West, has caused it to stop replacing its numbers and thus begin to disappear?

Just when I thought that with that barbed question I had finished for today, something occurs to me. John is upset because a father has, in his view, been grievously wronged by a court judgment. The judgment was, John tells us, in accordance with 'our central ethical system', as determined by the reigning ideology, whose ethics he considers profoundly unjust. Logically, then his complaint would be that of a citizen of, say, Communist Russia, unhappy that a court had made a judgment in accordance with the reigning, revolutionary ideology, rather than with natural justice or the traditional norms. It would be a complaint against the court in question. It would not be – not at least in the first instance, as with John's complaint – against the Communist media organs which very naturally support a judgment that upholds their ethical norms. But John spares the Irish High Court any direct criticism. Is this because there is in Irish law some legal prohibition on directly criticising a court judgment, or because John has accepted that conformity by the Irish courts to the reigning ideology goes literally without saying? I am puzzled, I don't know.

An Irish Camino de Santiago

Sunday 18 May
I had a response today by email to my article in *Ireland's Eye* about Slí Phádraig / St Patrick's Way. Some advice from Co. Sligo about the course the trail should take when heading through that county on the way to Lough Derg. A few weeks ago I travelled to Downpatrick and made a presentation of the idea to Tim Campbell at the St Patrick Centre there. I proposed to him that the Way should terminate at his Centre and in nearby Saul. I followed that up by writing the following piece for this month's *Ireland's Eye*, published in Mullingar and distributed throughout the country.

High Time to Create Slí Phádraig / St Patrick's Way

Many Irish people down the centuries and in recent years have walked a part or all of St James's Way, the *Camino de Santiago*. Traversing France from north to south, it continues along the north coast of Spain to the cathedral and tomb of St James in Santiago de Compostela. Ireland abounds in walking trails ranging from the 560-mile long Ulster Way to the Wicklow Way to the many walking trails of Cork and Kerry.

I think it is high time we had a Slí Phádraig / St Patrick's Way, passing through sites connected with the Saint's life. I mean a 'waymarked' way – with signs at suitable intervals indicating its course – and at each important site an information board explaining how that place was associated with the Saint. A specially published booklet would give details of the route, with accompanying little maps, and suggestions as to how the Way might be divided into walks of one day. Naturally, as with the *Camino de Santiago*, most people would not do the entire walk but parts of it of their own choosing; say, a one- or two-week stretch or a month's.

Given the international fame of St Patrick, Slí Phádraig would draw walkers from all over the world. Whatever about the route it might follow, the logical place for it to finish would be Saul and Downpatrick, two miles apart, where the Saint made his first convert, said his first Mass in Ireland, and where a large stone marks his grave. In Downpatrick there is already a handsome St Patrick interpretative centre run by a Northern Ireland body, the Friends of St Patrick, who could well be the organisers and sponsors of the entire Way.

To set the ball rolling, I imagine the St Patrick trail or pilgrim route starting at Drogheda, and flanking the Boyne to the Hill of Slane, where St Patrick lit the first Easter fire, which was seen from the Hill of Tara by the High King, Laogaire, From there it would proceed across Meath countryside to Tara, where the Saint had a confrontation with Laogaire and his druids.

The next direction would be west, heading for Croaghpatrick. Passing through Trim and Delvin, it might arrive at Multifarnham. Then it would be a matter of finding – I am not familiar with the area – a suitable route to the Shannon crossing at Lanesborough and on to Claremorris. I must look at *The Irish Coast to Coast Walk by Paddy Dillon*. The title intrigues me.

Along its entire length, the Way would avoid, as much as possible, roads with motorised traffic in favour of country tracks or open country where the farmers would feel honoured to have the Way cross their land. It would be necessary, moreover, at suitable intervals, for it to pass through or near towns or villages where the walkers could overnight..

From Claremorris, skirting the top end of Lough Mask, the Way would reach Croaghpatrick, where Patrick spent forty days fasting, fought victoriously against demons, and argued with an angel to extract promises for the Irish. Walkers in search of 'a genuine Patrick experience' might climb the Reek and obtain, weather permitting, fine views of Clew Bay. Or they might decide to reserve their energies for the trek through Westport northwards to the approximate site of the Forest of Foclut, south of Killala. It was thereabouts that the boy Patrick spent six years as a slave looking after his master's sheep.

I say 'approximate site' of the Forest of Foclut, because the forest no longer exists, and all that Patrick tells us about it in his Confession is that it was 'near the Western Sea'. But Tirechán, in his seventh-century Life of Patrick, indicates that it was just south of present-day Killala. At a well chosen spot there, an information board would inform the pilgrims and walkers of these facts. (There is general agreement today among Patrician scholars that it was hereabouts, rather than on Slemish in Co. Antrim, that Patrick spent those six years herding sheep.)

The next important St Patrick site is Lough Derg/St Patrick's Purgatory. in the southeast extremity of Co. Donegal. In 445 AD St Patrick spent some time in prayer and penance on the island in the lake. Subsequently, for centuries, a monastery stood there. In the Middle Ages the island became famous throughout Europe as the site of St Patrick's Purgatory on account of the many tales, told by visitors from afar, about the visions of hell, purgatory and heaven which they had seen in a cave there.

So from Ballina the Way would run east to Collooney, and on through Dromahair, past the south end of Lough Melvin and past Lower Lough Erne to Lough Derg. Here the walkers might choose to endure the three-day penitential rigours on the island. Or more likely, they might opt for simply enjoying the lovely view of the island church and march onwards, southeastwards, towards Armagh: the city where St Patrick established his bishop's seat, which became the ecclesiastical centre of Ireland..

How to traverse Co. Tyrone? Perhaps via Dromore and Augher. Is there a stretch of the Ulster Way which could be used here? In Armagh, Patrick's capital city so to speak, two St Patrick cathedrals face each other on their respective hills. Thereafter it would be a matter of the last leg or two running almost due east to Banbridge and to Saul/Downpatrick. Or perhaps an existing St Patrick's Trail through Newry might be used.

As I said, I am sketching out a possible route to set the ball rolling. I have put the idea to the Friends of St Patrick at the St Patrick Centre in Downpatrick, in the hope that they will take it up and convene an exploratory conference of tourism representatives from the County and District councils along the route.

Defining and signposting the Way would be a big work, in which local authorities could be persuaded to help. But while waiting to hear from the Centre, I would welcome advice and helpful comment from people living along the route I have sketched. Especially I would be glad to hear from regular hikers and from maintainers of local walking ways. Some existing local trails could possibly be used as parts of Slí Phádraig.

*

Concluding, I requested readers to 'send any relevant information, comments or advice either to the Editor or to me via my website.

WHERE IS THE EUROPEAN UNION HEADING?

Monday 19 May
At lunch-time I went to the Institute for International and European Affairs to hear a visiting gentleman from the EU hierarchy talk about 'Securing Other Europe: the European Union and Its Eastern Neighbours'. I hadn't previously heard the expression 'Other Europe'. It seems to be EU jargon for those countries to the east which are not members of the Union. I must make a correction. Having just glanced again at the notice for the meeting I see that the visiting gentleman was not 'from the EU hierarchy', but 'Mr Dov Lynch of the OSCE'. (Reflecting, I recall with some effort that OSCE stands for Organisation for Security and Co-operation in Europe.) I see further that 'Dov Lynch is currently the Senior Advisor to the Director General of the OSCE, and has previously held Research Fellow positions with both the Institute for Security Studies in Paris and Kings College, London'. Moreover, Mr Lynch's precise purpose today was to 'analyse the stakes for the EU in its relations with its eastern neighbours and offer an evaluation of the European Neighbourhood Policy (ENP) in the countries of the South Caucasus.' ENP is new to me, good that they spell it out.

I assumed that Mr Lynch was 'from the EU hierarchy' because of the title of his talk and the authority with which he spoke about EU interests and affairs. Noting now his present post in the OSCE and his previous institutional attachments, I realise that he is a member of that vague and multi-titled international bureaucracy which in ways unknown to us ordinary consumers influences, oversees, helps to direct and directs, the motions and doings of our great totalitarium. I imagine him moving across Europe and much farther afield – for the Organisation for Security and Co-operation in Europe, I recall, includes among its members, oddly, Canada, the USA and various states of Central Asia. I imagine him moving, understated and discreetly, dressed in good suits, from corridor of power to corridor of power, travelling first class, overnighting in top hotels or government residences, supported by a generous salary and paid expenses, occasionally giving paid talks and lectures in a network of publicly subsidised institutes such as ours here in Dublin, and all this financed by an international assortment of tax payers for whose well-being Mr

Dov Lynch works. By men such as Mr Lynch, in their various postings and gradings, with their varying degrees of decision-making powers, and under the vague oversight of mobile members or representatives of national governments from Canada to Kazakstan, we are ruled.

Mr Lynch talked a lot about Moldova and its breakaway enclave Transnistria, but he also dealt with Georgia, Bielorussia and Ukraine. He talked about conditions in these countries, their greater or lesser degree of democracy, their dispositions towards the EU, and EU initiatives with regard to them. His main ostensible concern, or rather that of the EU bureaucracy he was speaking about, was the 'stability' of these countries. The EU desired them 'stable', mainly in the sense of their having good neighbourly relations with the EU. But there was an underlying suggestion that it would be a good idea, and good for them and for the EU, if some day they would become members of the Union and thus pass under its sway. So that the 'securing' in the title of his talk acquired this secondary – or revealed its primary – meaning.

Two things struck me as he was speaking. First, that this snooping around the borders of Russia, and in territories which were until a few years ago within Russia's domain, would annoy Russia. Or rather, it would continue that provoking of Russia which had followed the collapse of Communism, when the EU and NATO, with American encouragement, had set to gobbling up, from Estonia to Bulgaria, as much of the previous Soviet empire as they could. And this continuing annoying of Russia would cause Russia to make more of those annoyed and bellicose noises which, in response to such previous encroachments, it has been making for some years past; with this in turn causing the western politicians and mass media to make more objecting noises about a revived Russian aggressiveness and imperialism! Was there some nostalgia in the EU and the West generally for the East-versus-West confrontation of the Cold War? Some insane urge to add that to the West's confrontation with radical Islam?

Second, and related to that, was the European Union incapable of settling down to be just itself? I mean, to concentrating on making the European Union a happy and prosperous unit of the world, coexisting with other units? Perhaps not. Perhaps, among its ruling elite, it has become an intrinsically unhappy thing that does not make sense, or rather that they believe can make sense only by extending its dominion horizontally and, by endless regulation, vertically. Is such a feeling of its being a formless senseless thing, regulating and grabbing in pursuit of sense, communicating itself downwards to those who are agitating on the No side in the Lisbon referendum?

In 1986, with the adhesion of Spain and Portugal, it became 12. Greece was already in. In 1993 it became a 'Union', and in 1995 Austria, Sweden and Finland joined, bringing it up to 15. In 2004, ten more countries, mostly ex-Soviet, acceded. Romania and Bulgaria followed in 2007. And now a whole host of Balkan countries is lined up for joining, with Turkey on the horizon.

For the decisive years of its formation, it was essentially a West European free-trade area. Under the leadership of Christian Democratic parties, a group of countries that had a history in common had agreed to form the European Economic Community. Certainly up to 1986, I felt, and I think most West Europeans felt, that it made a sort of sense. Leaving Greece aside, which did not impinge on our consciousness, it was roughly a territorial restoration of Charlemagne's empire, along with Britain and Ireland, as a free-trade area. They were the peoples – almost, only Austria was missing – whose ancestors had created the civilisation called 'Europe'. They constituted, historically and geographically, what 'Europe' had meant for centuries to the rest of the world. And the *raison d'être* of their being linked together was, to all appearances, free trade and free movement of people. It seemed to make sense. And it seemed that was how things would be thenceforth.

That was before I became aware – although the evidence was there in front of me – that Western Europe together with North America had abandoned European civilisation and was only geographically 'Europe'. But no matter, even with that, it still made sense enough; it was the space that Europe had occupied and where its memories and its material treasures were thick on the ground. But then, probably with America pushing them to grab, while the going was good, as much of the former Soviet dominions as they could, they became 'Europe of the Twenty-Seven', with nothing but the name of the continent to justify such a grouping. And the talk about including Turkey began because it was in NATO and America wanted it in. 'And why not Israel? Berlusconi said. 'It's already in the Eurovision pop song contest'. And others said, 'And what about those North African countries that have such close historical ties with France?' Now that I come to think of it, there is to be some kind of European Union peace-keeping military force in Chad, with Ireland contributing four hundred soldiers. Chad, south of Libya, for those who don't know.

As I listened to Mr Lynch, I asked myself was some imperialism of a new and infinite kind at work there. Of a new kind inasmuch as it was not a case of one nation, or the ruling class of one nation, or one great conqueror, wanting to rule more and more of the world, but rather a multi-ethnic bureaucracy wanting to do this, and not for a 'national' but for a merely ideological reason. The driving zeal seemed to be merely to spread further, and ever further, the post-European collection of liberal-consumerist values and rules of ultimately American inspiration, and the mode of mass life that followed from it. Then more nations, or rather, denationalised nations, would contribute more, lavishly paid bureaucrats to the multi-ethnic mix in Brussels, and more, lavishly paid deputies to the vast multi-ethnic and virtually powerless 'European Parliament' in Strasbourg and Brussels. Thus did deputies once travel from Vladivostok and Kirgistan and Kazakstan to the Supreme Soviet to be told what to approve. And with this growth of the multi-ethnic mix in Brussels and Strasbourg would come more sackfuls of money from the multi-ethnic consuming masses labouring through the checkouts in the supermarkets and shopping centres, as they spread like mushrooms across plains and mountains. Money which the Great Bureaucracy, under the assenting supervision of governments still antiquely called 'national', would allocate for this and that, in accordance with consumerist-liberal values and behavioural rules.

Incidentally, when I say there 'antiquely called "national"', I am not falling for the widely propagated story that 'the era of the nation-state has ended', nor suggesting that denationalised nations are becoming the new norm of the world. I used that phrase because the united-Europe enterprise since the start, as it lopped powers off European nation-states, has discouraged the national idea and, in particular, its expression as nationalism. But in so doing, it has by no means set a norm for the world in general. No doubt but that America, Japan, China and Russia remain great nation-states with flourishing nationalisms, do not apologise for it, and intend to remain that way. And remaining that way, they possess, each of them, a precious power which the construct that is now loosely called 'Europe' utterly lacks, namely, collective self-love, the love of the citizens for their shared community. The Europeans who are members of the Brussels construct may respect or favour it for practical reasons, but no one loves it. While the idealists who began its building, and those who followed them, were throwing cold water on Europe's nationalisms, and their disdain was taking effect, they omitted to foment a substitute pride in, and love for, the European community they said they were building.

A few weeks ago Brian Lenihan, Minister for Justice, spoke in this same institute about legal aspects of the Lisbon Treaty. At the start of his talk he said he believed that more must be done to make the Irish feel themselves 'part of Europe'. Because of my personal experience in this regard, his words took me aback. When he had finished, and there were questions and comments, I told him about that experience. Back in 1973, when I was living in Conamara, no one could have felt more European than I. It was not in the first place even a matter of feeling, so much as of knowing that Ireland and I were European – and of loving Europe as I loved Ireland. I believed, I said, that this unreflected sense of our being European was shared by many Irish people. A factor which had contributed greatly to this was the prominence then in our education system of the Irish language, with its Celtic dimension, and of the contribution by Irish monks and scholars to the founding of Europe.

Then came the referendum on our joining the European Economic Community and the government-supported campaign in favour of that. I noticed that the main campaign slogans of those who were advocating a Yes vote spoke of 'going into Europe'. We had 'no alternative, we must go into Europe because the UK was doing so!' I was offended. Who were these people, these Irish, who talked of our 'going into Europe'? Were they being tutored by some London public relations agency that made 'Europe' begin at Calais? So much did they offend me that I voted No. We joined, and increasingly after that the public language adopted the English habit of referring to what we had called 'the Continent' as 'Europe'. A final blow against my Irish sense of being European was the day I went to Dublin Airport and saw a large sign with an arrow indicating 'Flights to Europe'.

So I suggested to Mr Lenihan that in the matter of making the Irish feel 'part of Europe', it was a case of regaining ground that had been lost. He listened attentively and said that, with regard to the role of the education system, I had an important point. In fact, however, with regard to the Irish 'feeling themselves part of Europe', we may have been talking about different things.

Since those events of thirty-five years ago that I have just recounted,

'Europe' in Irish parlance has come to mean most of the time the European Union, the Brussels construct. This is the case, for instance, in the course of the current campaigning for and against the Lisbon Treaty. The No side reiterates that its criticisms of the Treaty do not mean that it is 'against Europe'; on the contrary, it maintains, it is 'for Europe'. As for myself, since I have come to see that in those thirty-five years Europe has rejected 'Europe' in the sense of European civilisation, I am no longer sure that my belief and feeling back then about 'Ireland in Europe' was based on an existing reality. Already in the 1970s what called itself Europe was a ghost of its historical self.

The Emptying Churches of Irish Catholicism

Tuesday 20 May
Eamon Maher has an article today in *The Irish Times* about the state of Catholic religion in the Republic. He is writing to mark the publication of a book of essays by various authors, *Contemporary Catholicism in Ireland: A Critical Appraisal*, which he and John Littleton edited. He writes:

> "One of the most remarkable developments of the past few decades has been the steady erosion of the majority Christian denomination in Ireland. Where once the Catholic Church played a vital (some might say unhealthy) role in the public and private lives of most of the population, we have now reached the stage where, for example, levels of practice in parts of Dublin are well below 10 per cent.
>
> The dearth of vocations to the priesthood and the ageing profile of most clergy have led to serious difficulties in running certain parishes. In addition, the emergence of an aggressive brand of secularism that is intolerant of opinions that do not coincide with the 'liberal agenda' has led to the marginalisation of those who hold on to deep religious beliefs.
>
> To speak openly about God or one's spiritual convictions will quite often elicit a bemused or even mocking response. There is no longer any social capital to be gained from being perceived to be a 'good Catholic'.
>
> Since the grossly inept (mis)handling of the revelations of child sexual abuse by a small number of priests in this country, the hierarchy seem demoralised and incapable of offering the type of prophetic witness that is needed to win back lost ground.
>
> In his latest book, *Global Ireland: Same Difference*, Tom Inglis argues that the Irish have become the same as their western counterparts in their fascination with the material world, their pursuit of pleasure and their obsession with self: 'They [the Irish] have moved from being quiet, poor Catholic Church mice embodying a discourse and practice of piety and humility, to becoming busy, productive self-indulgent rats searching for the next stimulation'.
>
> The Irish have definitely changed, and not only in their attitude to religion. We are more self-confident (brash?), prosperous, cosmopolitan, liberal than we were a few decades ago. But in our blind pursuit of the pleasures of this world is there not a danger that we have lost sight of some of the positive aspects of religion?"

He continues, but that is the essence of what he says and it contains nothing that is entirely new to me. Nothing except that quoted description of the Irish today as 'busy, productive self-indulgent rats searching for the next stimulation', which to say the least is an inaccurate and insulting generalisation. But I will read the book which Maher has co-edited, and to which his article today is only an introduction. In my years in Italy I became out of touch with those aspects of Irish Catholicism which do not make headlines. When I wrote the pamphlet *Savvy and the Preaching of the Gospel* a few years ago, in response to Vincent Twomey's *The End of Irish Catholicism?*, it was based only on material I found in Twomey's book and from information occasionally gleaned from sporadic sightings of the Irish mass media.

I continue to be struck by something that struck me then. Although regular practice of Catholicism is considerably less in Italy than even today in the Republic of Ireland, the Catholic religion is much more in evidence there than here. Also, as an offshoot of that, there is much more public recognition of many people's belief in the existence of a spiritual world, and of the pursuit of holiness, as elements of life past and present. In part this has to do with the strong persistence in Italy of a Catholic culture in the form of town and city festivals, mostly in honour and commemoration of a dead saint, or to mark some Church holyday such as the Assumption of the Blessed Virgin. All of these festivals are enacted or participated in by thousands of people or, as in Catania for the feast of Saint Agatha, by an entire large city. Our ruinous history, by one means or another, deprived us of such a normal heritage of a Catholic people. Indeed, St Patrick's Day apart, our special public holidays are days when the banks are closed. If ever there were a parody of a capitalist society!

Moreover, in Italy, in these great public religious occasions, the civic authorities actively participate. I remember when, in the few public manifestations of Catholic religion which we had in Ireland in my youth, such participation by the civic authorities was commonplace. But I have the impression that the anti-Catholic liberal blight of recent years, which Eamon Maher refers to, has put an end to that.

Even when public manifestation of religion was usual in Ireland, it was, I think, a departure from an acquired conviction of most Irish Catholics – men in particular – that their religion belonged in a private and family sphere, and not in the civic or political sphere. A sort of inherited Catholic secularism that arose from the experience of having long survived as Catholics – I speak of the post-Reformation centuries – in an environment where the civic authority was hostile, or at least unfriendly. In Italy, on the contrary, the degree of public cultural identification with the Catholic heritage on the part even of non-believers holding civic authority can bring an Irishman up short. In the town where I was living, forty minutes by train from Rome, the town council, shortly before Easter Week, puts up posters advertising the times of the Easter Week ceremonies in the town's churches.

There are a couple of other reasons for the greater evidence of religion and the spiritual in Italian life. The television channels cover the big religious festivals as news. As part of their normal programming, they give occasional notable space to dramas and documentaries with religious themes. These may deal with Padre Pio – who has a mass cult among all types and classes – or St Bernadette of Lourdes or some priest, monk, nun or other man or woman, who in recent times in Italy was notable for holiness and good works. Rather than being shown in tv dramas and documentaries only as amusing Father Teds or as pederasts, priests, when they figure, are mostly shown as all adults, Italian or Irish, know most of them to be: conscientious ministers of God. In other words, Italian television treats religion and the spiritual as Irish television does not: as an important part of the country's life and culture. And finally, due largely to the fact that the Pope lives effectively, if not politically, in Italy, there is ample coverage in the news bulletins of his significant statements and actions. I nearly forgot: there are also two daily, officially Catholic newspapers, *Avvenire* and *L'Osservatore Romano*, the former speaking for the bishops, the latter for the Vatican. And all this in a country where relatively few people are regular Mass-goers, where daily life is not obviously marked by religion, many prominent people declare themselves *laici* or non-believing secularists, and anti-clerical utterances are commonplace.

I find all that simply adult; as if Italy were saying by its public actions, its new books and its mass media: Look, *in relation to religion and the spiritual, we are various*. By contrast, since I returned here, it seems to me as if the Republic were saying by its public behaviour and its mass media: *With regard to religion and the spiritual, we won't let you see*. According to the 2006 census, there were 3,681,400 Catholics in the Republic. They were 86.8 per cent of its total population. The official figure for Catholics in all of Ireland is nearly four and a half million out of a population of nearly six million.

Apart from my knowledge that there is an obscuring of ourselves to ourselves at work here, I feel this collective life around me as an imprisonment of my humanity in a house with a low ceiling where my housemates are involved in a game of 'Let's pretend': 'Let's pretend that reality is entirely material, and all concerns and passions likewise.'

In an interview in *The Irish Times* a few weeks ago the Archbishop of Dublin, Diarmuid Martin, said that, while recent surveys in the Republic had indicated that about 44 per cent of self-proclaimed Catholics go to Mass, he believes that the true figure is close to half of that. Dublin, with a Catholic population of 1.04 million, is one of the largest archdioceses in either Britain or Ireland. It extends over an area of 170km by 80km, taking in all of Co. Dublin, almost all of Co. Wicklow, much of Co. Kildare, as well as parishes in counties Carlow, Wexford and Laois. It has 238 churches, including our church here in Maynooth. In its 200 parishes 731 priests serve the faithful.

'The church in Dublin is middle-class,' said Archbishop Martin. 'Priests in some urban working-class parishes are reporting weekly Mass attendances of 3-5 per cent. Average figures for Dublin are in the region of 20-25 per cent.' He is struck, he said, by the relatively small number of young people who attend church services. 'I can go to parishes on a Sunday where I find no person in the congregations between the ages of 16 and 36. An age-filled church is not a good thing. The biggest challenge is the rebuilding of contact with the younger generation, who are a great generation '.

The average age of priests serving in Dublin today is sixty-three. The retirement age is seventy-five, which means that, if current trends continue, as many as 50 per cent of all priests in the archdiocese will no longer be serving within a decade. The archbishop envisages a future where priests 'will be freed up to preach the word of God and celebrate the sacraments'; this, because he estimates there are twenty types of ministry which could be undertaken by lay faithful. Most of this work would be voluntary, in areas such as pastoral care, administration, and child protection. 'The primary objective is to help the young to be open to the transcendent. To go beyond the self. Parishes must become involved in support faith groups for the young'. 'In general', said the Archbishop concluding, 'the archdiocese has to have a much more evangelical outreach'.

In May 1962 *Doctrine and Life* published an article of mine, 'Will the Irish Stay Christian?' I was discussing the possibility that what has in fact happened *could* happen. I could now write 'and thus it has come to pass'. At the time, my title was considered so provocative that the very enlightened Dominican editor, Fr Austin Flannery, considered it prudent to replace it with 'Ireland and Christianity' in the listing of articles on the cover. I had returned the year before from a year spent in then famously 'pagan' Sweden. Reading back in Swedish history, I had been struck by how ardently, in the late nineteenth century, questions of faith and ritual in the Lutheran state church had been debated in public. Sweden was still then, in open profession and in practice, a Christian nation. Could the same transition happen in the near future in Catholic Ireland? I dared to ask. It was at that time, for sensible people generally, an unimaginable development. The reason why it seemed possible to me, apart from that Swedish precedent, was the nature of Catholic belief in Ireland as I observed it. Generally, but most strikingly in men, it was more of a belief that what the Church–specifically the clergy– taught was true and right than of a direct, personal belief in Jesus Christ or loyalty to him. There was an absence of that personal appropriation of the Christian faith and worldview such as I had observed in many Protestants and, indeed, in German Catholics.

Archbishop Martin has said more than once that in the present situation in Dublin the Church needs to be, or rather to become, evangelising. And I think he is right, and not only with regard to Dublin. It means not taking for granted in the people, as forty years ago one could do, any Christian faith or knowledge. Bringing Christ and the Church to them, as if they had never heard of them – even when still, in most instances, they actually have. Such evangelisation might in part take the occasional form of 'soap box' addresses outside supermarkets and the like. But I think that the fundamental occasion for it is the Sunday Mass, simply because it is the regular and well known weekly occasion when the teaching Church presents itself to the rest of the Church and to people generally.

In the good old days people attended Sunday Mass partly because as Catholics they believed it was their moral duty to do so, and partly through conformity, because almost everyone else was doing so. The latter of those two motivations no longer exists, the former only to a small degree. Consequently, in order that the Sunday Mass be made an instrument of evangelisation – drawing non-practising, poorly instructed and lapsed Catholics as well as more or less fervent and instructed Catholics – it must be made an intrinsically *attractive* event. Attractive in the dual sense of drawing physically and holding mentally and emotionally.

I have thought about how this might be done. But let me preface my remarks on that by saying the following. There have been two occasions on which I have seen our parish church in Maynooth packed: every seat filled, and people standing along the walls and at the back. One was the Stations of the Cross on Good Friday at three in the afternoon, the other a First Communion ceremony on a Sunday morning. I realised that both these church services, which were so clearly attractive in the literal sense of 'drawing people', shared three qualities that made them so. First, they were, in a general way if not in all particulars, profoundly intelligible. The people who attended them knew exactly what the services were about and what their purpose was. And they understood the significance of the principal rituals performed. Second, they considered the event that each of the services marked or enacted important to them personally. Finally, both services by reason of their eloquent symbolism and ritual, had a dramatic or theatrical dimension. As a consequence of their having those three qualities, it was virtually certain that, when repeated the following year, they would prove equally attractive. Reflecting on this, I realised that for the ordinary Sunday Mass to be maximally attractive, in the full sense of physically drawing, and mentally and emotionally holding, it would need to have those same qualities to the greatest degree possible.

The principal requirement is intelligibility in every dimension of that concept. Many people naively thought that the decision forty odd years ago to have the Mass said in the vernacular rather than in Latin would achieve intelligibility; but that is far from being the case, even when the congregation consists of well informed Catholics with good hearing ability. Intelligibility has of course to do with more than the spoken word, but it is the basic factor. To the degree that what is spoken from the altar by the priest or the readers cannot be understood in every part of the church, to that degree the Mass is unintelligible and a source of irritation or boredom rather than devotion.

But let us imagine that I am the sort of person who might possibly be evangelised, someone to whom the faith has yet to be brought: a nominal Catholic or an unbeliever. And let us assume that for one reason or another I enter a church just before Sunday Mass is about to begin; a church, moreover, where care has been taken that all words spoken from the altar area can be clearly heard in every part of it. The first thing I need is that, when the priest appears and greets the people, he says in a few words – not more than ten – what is the nature and purpose of this service that is about to begin: what it is that 'we' are about to do together. (To save brain-wracking labour for ordinary priests, the Bishops' Liturgy Commission could draft a suitable form of words for this, and distribute it to the priests of Ireland.)

It would also help me greatly if I could read the texts that the priest is reading, or reciting off by heart, as well as the texts that the appointed 'readers' are reading aloud. Some churches in the Dublin archdiocese supply Mass-books to the congregation, others, probably the majority, 'missalettes' – leaflets giving the text of the Mass of that Sunday. The latter are more satisfying for the congregation, on condition that they include all the texts used on that particular day (not all of them do). The Mass-books, which contain texts for many Sundays, do not indicate which Sunday of the Church year this particular Sunday is, and require the priest at the start of the Mass to announce this, or a printed notice to make it known. They are, moreover, divided into sections for texts that are always used, texts peculiar to this Sunday, and texts of Eucharistic Prayers and Canons that are used on some Sundays but not on all. So to use them, someone like the man I am imagining myself to be, and indeed regular Mass-goers, would require guidance from the celebrating priest if they are to be used properly. So the Mass leaflets are indeed more serviceable, provided, as I said, that they contain all the texts used on that particular Sunday.

The readings – the texts read aloud by the 'readers' – have been written by persons long dead whom someone like me has seldom or perhaps never heard of. So I would like a few explanatory words to accompany the mention of any of these persons' names. For St Paul, for instance, 'an important missionary to communities of early Christians in the eastern Mediterranean and in Rome'. For St. Peter, 'the fisherman whom Jesus Christ appointed head of the early Church'. For Isaiah, 'a prophet or inspired preacher to the Jewish people in the eighth century before Christ'. (Here again the Liturgy Commission could establish and distribute standard forms of words.) At first, perhaps these 'superfluous' descriptions might sound odd to well-informed Catholics, but they would become accustomed to them as they become accustomed to, say, 'George Bush, President of the United States'.

Moreover, if there is a set of circumstances knowledge of which would enrich understanding of the text to be read, it would help if the reader prefaced his or her Reading with a few prepared, explanatory words. And of course, what I have said about the Readings applies also to the priest's introduction of the Gospel of the day. A final suggestion about the Readings: my ordinary man's ears are offended by words such as 'Ephesians, Thessalonians, Corinthians'. What is meant – and if so why not say it? – is 'the early Christian community at Ephesus, Salonica or Corinth', as the case may be.

I am as susceptible to the fascination of ritual–any sort of ritual – as anyone. So if this Sunday Mass I have dropped into is to fascinate and hold me, and perhaps make me want to return another Sunday, nothing could be more effective than its being performed expressly as a ritual or, if you like, as theatre. The last thing which the physical movements of the priest and the readers, of the bringers of the Offertory gifts, of the distributors of Communion and so on, should be is casual. Make them thought through, practised in advance, utterly formal; the same movements always performed in the same studied manner.

A final word. If I have had a good experience at a Sunday Mass, remind me, visibly, as I pass by the church on weekdays, that I can have it again. On a special notice-board erected in front of the church, and in easily readable lettering, affix a notice each week announcing a Reading and the Gospel for the following Sunday. In this manner: 'NEXT SUNDAY. **If you stop sinning, you will live**. By the prophet Ezekiel. **Making good use of your talents**. By St Matthew.' Not only will it remind me: it may well make someone else, as clueless as myself, curious about what goes on in there of a Sunday; curious enough to explore.

The Ghost Of Europe

Wednesday 21 May
When I wrote a couple of days ago that what called itself Europe in the 1970s was already a ghost of its historical self, I meant a ghost in two senses. Along with the USA and following its lead, the Europe of history, in effect Western Europe, was replacing its European civilisation with a new collection of rules. At the same time, in structure and external impact, it was ceasing to be what it had been historically: a latterday equivalent of Ancient Greece, a group of autonomous peoples who, sharing a distinctive common worldview and often at war, developed a life and a great civilisation which impinged on other peoples.* It was becoming, what it remains, a politically unified plurality living by post-European rules; at peace, without impact on the world; and using a culture derived from elsewhere as its shared contemporary culture.

That this was and is a ghost or afterlife of Europe is obvious. That out of it– its material and its need for sense being human – a new civilisation could spring is possible. But that is impossible while this group of peoples remains without any shared historical event of note since the Second World War; with no common, marking experience to look back to since that; and with the memory and disgrace of that lying heavily on them. A common defence against an attack from outside would free them from this incubus. But more likely, and less painful as a liberation, is the social chaos that will involve them all when the American socio-ethical experiment that has been holding them captive collapses.

---

* See my *The Revision of European History*, p. 51.

The Illegible Treaty of Lisbon

Friday 30 May
There is frequent reference in the referendum campaigns to the illegibility, meaning unintelligibility, of the Lisbon Treaty. It is long, written in dense legalese and packed with 'references' to other documents and treaties. A few days ago the Irish Commissioner of the European Union, Charles McCreevy, in Ireland on a visit, was heard to say on radio: 'I wouldn't expect any sane, sensible Irish person to read the Treaty from cover to cover' but [.....] it is good for Ireland and everyone should vote Yes'. In *Phoenix* just out today, in the 'funny' section, there is an item headed 'Life destroyed for man who claims to understand the Treaty', along with a photo of a bespectacled gormless youth. The text reads:

> "'A man who claims to have read the Lisbon Treaty twice and 'understands it perfectly', has been branded 'a fantasist and egocentric' by workmates. The man, who works in an unclosed factory in Tipperary says his life has become 'a living hell' since he read up on the Treaty and he may be forced to leave the locality .
> 'Nobody believes a word I say any more. My credibility is shot to pieces', said the man yesterday. 'My fiancée finished with me, because she said she couldn't trust anyone who would make such wild assertions. She practically accused me of being a drug addict'. One work colleague said the man was 'obviously trying to impress people but went too far. He needs help'."

In fact, however, and mercifully to all concerned, we are not actually being asked to say Yes or No to the document itself, but to a moderately long, composite Amendment to the Irish Constitution which adherence to the Lisbon Treaty would necessitate. Saying Yes to this would mean, at one remove, saying Yes to the Treaty. The proposed Amendment, the Twenty-Eighth, would insert six subsections into Article 29. The first two of these subsections are as follows:

> 'The State may ratify the Treaty of Lisbon amending the Treaty on European Union and the Treaty establishing the European Community, signed at Lisbon on the 13th day of December 2007, and may be a member of the European Union established by virtue of that Treaty.
> No provision of this Constitution invalidates laws enacted, acts done or measures adopted by the State that are necessitated by the obligations of membership of the European Union referred to in subsection 10 of

this section (i.e. above) or prevents laws enacted, acts done or measures adopted by the said European Union or by institutions thereof, or by bodies competent under the treaties referred to in this section, from having the force of law in the State.'

That seems to mean a final subordination of our Constitution to the European Union. But this is not, at least not explicitly, the main issue being raised by the No side. Libertas – the ad hoc campaigning body founded by Declan Ganley – Sinn Féin, Cóir, and others on the No side, are arguing for No on more specific grounds. 'The EU Courts can decide that anything in this Treaty means anything the EU bureaucrats want. Our low business taxes will be abolished in the name of European "harmonisation". We will be forced to legalise abortion. The EU, which is already building a European army, will disregard Irish neutrality and make Irishmen fight in its wars. Lisbon will reduce the voting weight of Ireland in the Council of Ministers and deprive us of a Commissioner for periods of five years. The powers of Brussels in sixty key policy areas will be extended. Vote NO. Don't Be Bullied. Ireland Can Do Better. Vote NO. People Died for Our Freedom. Vote NO'. Two or three of those allegations of what Lisbon would mean are mere suppositions or based on flimsy grounds, but this is politics.

The No side also makes the point that the Netherlands and France voted No to the first version of the Lisbon Treaty, called the European Constitution, and that if referendums on Lisbon were permitted in the other twenty-six member states of the Union, it is likely that in most of them the vote would be No. (In the other member states there is no constitutional obligation to ratify a 'Treaty' by referendum – clever move to rename it a 'Treaty'! – so Lisbon is being ratified by their parliaments.)

GOODBYE TO TERRY KEANE

Wednesday 4 June
Terry Keane died last Saturday. Yesterday I went to the removal at Glasthule church and today to the funeral. A scarlet woman for the nation, for me she was a dear friend, a vivacious, intelligent and insightful woman who enriched my life. Among other things, she enriched it by a few times telling me truths about myself.

Why do I associate her mainly with the 'Sixties, when as it happens I was in touch with her on and off after that for many years and lunched with her a few weeks ago? Because it was in the 1960s that she first hit Dublin, and her vivacity, *sournoiserie*, wit and sexiness – and her charming English alienness – were perfectly in tune with that exciting, exotic decade. Essentially, she belongs for me in the *early* 60s when, returned from Sweden, I intended to 'settle down' and was in search of a girl to marry. The poles of my life then were my cottage in Dundrum, art exhibitions where I did my critic's work, and the New Amsterdam café where young swinging Dublin, when it wasn't elsewhere drinking *mateus rosé*, was becoming familiar with *espresso* coffee.

I am moved still to recall that, when a thoughtless episode had made her pregnant, she had the confidence in me to come to my cottage and ask could she escape from people by staying there until the birth. I am touched still by the naiveté of it in a woman who was so worldly-wise. Could she not guess that, if I hadn't asked her to marry me, I might want to ask someone else and that my cottage was, so to speak, my base of operations? Instead she went to London, and her daughter Jane, born and adopted there, joined her years later, after she had married Ronan Keane and had her other children.

Because I was away at the time, I have never been entirely clear about the circumstances of her 'coming out' on *The Late Late Show* with regard to her long affair with Charlie Haughey. But I have gathered that it happened on her initiative; that she went to Gay Byrne with the story when my son Cilian was producer on the show. And she did it because Haughey, beset by tribunals of enquiry, had decided it was best to clear his decks and had sent back to her anything that connected them. I have heard, too, that she followed it up by writing a long account of the twenty-seven-year affair in *The Sunday Times*; an account accompanied by photographs of the pair, and for which she got paid a lot of money. Cliché-style furious behaviour of a woman scorned, which I am sorry that Terry sank to, and for which, I hear, she apologised publicly a few years ago. But I do not understand why, as a result of her telling the story publicly, she became in Dublin what the priest in his funeral homily today called a 'pariah'.

My goodness, in the Dublin of today an affair with another woman's husband is hardly so out of the ordinary. Nor was it a revelation to Haughey's wife, who had known about it for years and who was, indeed, occasionally in touch with Terry about him. I am not going to say that 'everyone knew about it', but a lot of people did. It was not something you whispered, and the repeated weighted references to 'Sweetie' in Terry's social-gossip column in the *Sunday Independent* were, I thought, clear enough. Those who knew of it, knew that the pair of them usually met abroad, when Haughey was abroad on official business. But occasionally they could be seen together in Dublin in a restaurant or a night club. And I recall a lunch outdoors with Terry and three of her girlfriends, with a large and beautiful floral wreath occupying the centre of the table. Without saying his name, Terry made very clear whom the wreath was from; and some way or other, then or later, I heard that it cost £200. He was always generous with her.

One memory I have of Terry's kindness to me has to do with his generosity in another direction. She knew that, in the 1970s, living in Conamara with my wife and children, I had fallen on hard times and was unable to find work. She passed on the word to Charlie and a call reached me to come to his office in Dublin. He was sitting at the desk with his basilisk stare. He opened a drawer and took out a brown envelope. 'I have always been interested in the subject of nationalism', he said. 'I've heard you're working on that. I'd like you to do me a report'. And he passed me the envelope, which I later found contained £100.

With Charlie's generosity, it was a matter of to each, if not his due, at least what suited the person and the occasion. To selected housewives in his constituency every Christmas, it was a Christmas hamper. Some will say, of course, that the money he spent generously on others wasn't his; that he got most of it from his rich businessmen friends. But it was still his to do as he liked with. And I reject the continuing efforts of his enemies in *The Irish Times* and the South Dublin bourgeoisie to bury his memory in a mire of 'corruption'. The best efforts of the tribunals of enquiry did not in fact show that he did any favours in return for the millions which that coterie of Irish businessmen gave him. That he did not pay the due income tax, but had to be brought later to pay it, reflects simply how he felt himself above the norm – and was encouraged so to feel himself.

What happened there was, I believe, a special and symbolic moment in modern Irish history. For the first time since the Revolution a number of ordinary Catholic Irishmen were, buccaneer-like, amassing through commercial and financial dealings great wealth. Recognising in Haughey one of their own background who had aristocratic pretensions, and trusting him to do both himself and themselves proud, they fed him the wherewithal for generous giving and splendid living. They were his courtiers, if you like, and he their king. They were celebrating through him both themselves and their shared good fortune. And his own generous giving apart, he did do them proud with his Gandon mansion, his racehorses, his handmade shirts from Paris, his private island off the Kerry coast, his motor yacht, his hawking, and his attempt to reintroduce in Kerry the White-Tailed Eagle. Naturally, for those of the new South Dublin bourgeoisie who felt themselves a cut above the common Irish they had sprung from, all this went far beyond what befitted a commoner, and a Northsider to boot. It made their own ambitious keeping up with the Jones's petty by comparison, and Charles Haughey, consequently, anathema to them.

Haughey did some mean and some cruel things in his political life, as what politician doesn't? In each successive ministry that he held, he was innovative, compassionate, did public good. His vanity and arrogance prevented him from welding his party into a dependable unity, so that he never got that stable, long stretch as taoiseach that he craved. But his short periods as taoiseach he used well; both in the matter of the North, and ultimately, in the matter of the economy, where he laid the basis for the Celtic Tiger.

He used those short periods fruitfully in another way too; namely, to practise in the public sphere, as he did in the private sphere, that virtue which Aristotle in his *Ethics* calls *magnificence*. He names it there as one of the virtues proper to a rich man. Writing in the context of Ancient Greece, he applied it only to the man rich in private resources; but it applies equally in our well-taxed days to the man rich in public resources, provided the expenditure is in the public interest. Granted the originating impulses may have come from various quarters, it was Haughey who took the executive decisions that in Dublin restored the Royal Hospital in Kilmainham; made Government Buildings splendid; revivified Temple Bar; and established the International Financial Services Centre and the Irish Museum of Modern Art. He was, besides, the first leading member of government since Independence to give artists the feeling that the State cherished them: whether by relieving them of income tax in 1967, by establishing Aosdána in 1991, or by his general comportment throughout his life towards artists and the arts.

I was not intending to write about Charlie, except in relation to Terry. I find I have gone far beyond that. But Terry, whom I will miss from this world, and who I pray will be happy forever in that other world, will understand.

The Campaigns Rage

Thursday 5 June
There is a Referendum Commission which, among other things is supposed to clarify the Lisbon Treaty for the voting consumers. At a press conference two days ago, its chairman, a judge, was queried on a point of detail by a journalist. After a pause and a rifling through papers – I heard it on radio – he attempted an answer, then said the matter was not very clear and attempted another answer. Finally he said the Referendum Commission would look into the matter and report back. Yesterday, again on radio, a journalist, the station's specialist on the Treaty, said the second answer had been wrong and explained why, quoting from the Treaty. He also pointed out what he said were discrepancies between a general explanatory document published by the Commission and a Government White Paper on the subject published some time ago. And so it goes on.

Today an opinion poll in *The Irish Times* shows a huge advance for the No vote since the last poll. No is now 35%, Yes 30%, the rest undecided. When you take into account that all the big political parties, some big trade unions, the main farmers' organisations, and the main businessmen's organisations have advocated Yes – and the Catholic bishops have made a discreetly supportive statement – something strange seems to be happening. The analysis accompanying the poll result says that the main reasons for the decisions to vote No are inability to understand what the Treaty is proposing, a desire to keep 'Ireland's power and identity', and a desire to safeguard our military neutrality. Women are considerably more against than for. The only social classes where the Yes side is ahead is what is called the ABC1 – the rich and powerful.

I feel myself that the No side is above all an emotional rejection, perhaps the last rebellion of Irish nationalism. Now that, on account of our new wealth, the European Union has ceased to be a supplier of big subsidies to the Republic, people's dislike of the minute intrusiveness or regulationism of 'Brussels' is coming to the fore. Often in these last years you hear objections to this in the form of complaints about 'the amount of paperwork': from farmers, fishermen, builders and artisan food producers (to name only categories whose complaints I have personally heard). The attitude has been, while groaning about it, to accept it ultimately as a distasteful, time-consuming imposition of the good times. Now it is feeding an awakened general feeling on the No side that the Union is an oppressive force. Of course de Tocqueville, in 1840, foresaw regulationism as he foresaw everything. He wrote:

> 'After having thus successfully taken each member of the community in its powerful grasp, and fashioned them at will, the supreme power...covers the surface of society with network of small, complicated rules, minute and uniform, through which the most original minds and the most energetic characters cannot penetrate, to rise above the crowd. The will of man is not shattered, but softened, bent and guided; men are seldom forced to act, but they are constantly restrained from acting.
>
> Such a power does not destroy, but it prevents existence; it does not tyrannise, but it compresses, enervates, extinguishes and stupefies a people, until each nation is reduced to nothing better than a flock of timid and industrious animals, of which the government is the shepherd.'

He could well be describing the later phases of the Roman Empire, but in fact he was describing the ultimate outcome of liberal democracy. No one in the No campaign is being as eloquent as he about the EU regulationism or its societal impact, nor indeed is it being mentioned much expressly. But the suppressed fury and sense of humiliation that it has generated in many hard-working people is doubtless fuelling the talk of real or imaginary oppressions, or threats of oppression, that the No side is engaging in.

The Yes side has a difficult job to do. Consisting essentially of 'the Establishment', it has many good concrete reasons for supporting whatever the EU establishment has decided is the best way forward for the EU. For the politicians, top civil servants and Brussels lobbyists, it means continuing to belong to a club which they have become used to and whose ways and aims they substantially approve of.

The club provides interesting foreign travel; for some of them very lucrative careers or the prospect of such careers; and for some, again, the pleasure of shaping the lives of hundreds of millions of people for their good. Businessmen and farmers who import or export; professionals of various kinds who belong to professional associations that span Europe; men and women generally who find Ireland too small an arena for their talents; liberal ideologues who look to Brussels to continue its work of reforming and 'modernising' Irish *mores* – all these, too, have very good concrete reasons for voting Yes. And in all or at least most of these instances, what is true for the individuals in question, is true also for the voters in their families.

But these good concrete motives for voting Yes are not such as the Establishment spokespersons can present to the electorate as reasons for voting Yes. The arguments they can use are quite limited. Mainly, they can say, as they are in fact saying, that the EU, under that name or earlier names, has contributed much to Irish wellbeing, prosperity and presence in the world, and that this Treaty is essentially about making the EU – specifically the enlarged, 27-member EU – function more efficiently. They can also say that by introducing the possibility of petitions to the European Parliament signed by one million people, Lisbon will make the EU more democratic. But in fact they find themselves, for the most part, arguing for Yes by refuting the No side's many allegations of the dire consequences of a Yes vote. And that is not the best possible of debating stances.

Moreover, as things are shaping, with the No side mobilising voters against 'a bullying EU elite' that pursues its own interests regardless of what the people want, the Irish Establishment's stance for Yes tends to merge them with that elite and make this target a dual one.

Sorting Out Art in Dublin

Friday 6 June
As a boy attending Belvedere College, I occasionally took my lunch sandwiches to Dublin's Municipal Gallery of Modern Art a few hundred metres away on Parnell Square.[1] It was there in that lunch-hour stillness, moving from picture to picture, that I developed an emotional attachment to the painted image which has persisted through my life. The paintings were mainly Irish, with some French and English, dating from the 1860s to the early 1940s. The Gallery's collection had grown from Sir Hugh Lane's large gift of pictures to Dublin – three hundred or so – a hundred years ago this year. Word has been out recently that the Gallery is having a big exhibition to mark that centenary, and believing that it had already opened I went there today.

Everyone has heard of the dispute between London and Dublin about thirty-nine of the Lane paintings – mostly French works – which were originally included in that gift to Dublin. On the basis of a contested interpretation of Sir Hugh's Will, London's National Gallery claimed them. But a complicated compromise was arrived at in the 1970s whereby an alternating four of a specific eight, plus another four paintings, would be exhibited in London, while the rest were held on loan in Dublin. A big point in the advance publicity for this exhibition has been that, to mark the special occasion, all thirty-nine will once again be shown together in Dublin.

It turned out that the exhibition has not yet opened – it will open later this month – but it is already substantially in place. It consists, I discovered, of 185 pictures that formed the founding exhibition of the Gallery of Modern Art in Clonmell House, Harcourt Street in 1908. It was the first public gallery in Europe devoted specifically to 'Modern Art'. For the most part the pictures were donated by Sir Hugh Lane himself, but there were also some works contributed by artists sympathetic to his enterprise. Together, they formed a fairly representative collection of paintings by contemporary Irish, French and British artists.

---

[1] Its full name was The Hugh Lane Municipal Gallery of Modern Art. In 2002 it changed its name to 'Dublin City Gallery. The Hugh Lane'.

I had come principally to see the famous '39 Continental Pictures'– as the group in question are called – finally reunited in Dublin. I assumed that Hugh Lane had regarded them as the jewels of the collection he donated. To my great surprise and disappointment, I discovered that they were not being exhibited together, on their own, but mingled here and there with the other paintings in the exhibition. A one-page leaflet informed visitors where they were to be found. They were hung in eight different rooms of the eighteen rooms being used for the exhibition. A man and woman who had come all the way from Co. Down to see 'the Thirty-Nine' were as disappointed as I was. I looked at the Courbet, the Renoir and the Manet in Room 17 and the three Corots in Room 12 and a couple of Courbets in Room 13, and left it at that. A number of the other painters of the Thirty-Nine didn't interest me enough, as painters, to go to the trouble of traipsing around to find them. It was the sight of the thirty-nine together, and the conclusions I might draw from that, that I was looking forward to. But that sight I could not have.

It was years since I had last been in the Gallery. Apart from some new rooms, a bookshop, and some Irish paintings from the 1960s and 70s added, I noticed several things I had not seen before. There was a special darkened cubicle for stained glass which illuminated the works shown. The biggest of them was Harry Clarke's "Eve of St Agnes" and there was a work by Mainie Jellett. A substantial section on the ground floor was given over to Francis Bacon. It contained his studio (donated by his heir and transported from London) : a few finished and unfinished paintings, mostly of human figures done in Bacon's usual mutilating manner; and a room with seats where you could watch a continuously playing video of him being interviewed.

His studio was visible through glass. It was a scene of crammed disorder with very little space left free. A notice told me that 7,000 items had been found in it. Three touch-screens on a wall provided 'an edited version of the Francis Bacon Studio Database'. 'The complete database', it continued, 'is the first computerised archive of the entire contents of an artist's studio. It has entries on circa 570 books and catalogues, 1500 photos, 100 slashed canvases, 1300 leaves torn from books, 2000 artist's materials and 70 drawings.' By following instructions on a touch-screen you could call up an image and a descriptive text for any one of the items its computer contained. I called up a torn-out page, a couple of photos and a half-used tube of paint. Clearly, this Bacon section was for Bacon cultists, rather than ordinary art-loving human beings.

Elsewhere, in the new part of the Gallery, there was a 'Scully Room', containing four framed paintings of variously coloured rectangular panels; one colour per panel. Immediately I saw Mondrian of sixty or seventy years ago, except that these panels had scruffily finished edges whereas Mondrian's were geometrically sharp. It seemed odd to have this special 'Scully Room', when there was no special room for any other painter and the works shown added nothing of aesthetic value to the Gallery. Having only vaguely heard of Scully, I have just googled him and learn that he is 'an Irish-born American painter and printmaker who has twice been named a Turner Prize nominee' and 'his work is in major museums worldwide'. I note that one of these is the Irish Museum of Modern Art (the one in Kilmainham, Dublin) and that in 2006 'Scully donated eight of his paintings to 'the Hugh Lane Gallery in Dublin, which opened an extension in May 2006 with a room dedicated to Scully's works.'

In a separate, upstairs part of the Gallery there was an exhibition called *'Other Men's Flowers'*. A notice explained as follows:

> "Taken from a quote by French moralist Montaigne, "in this book I have only made up a bunch of other men's flowers, providing of my own only the string that ties them together", *other men's flowers* draws on the collections of The Tate and The Hugh Lane as well as the private collections of the artists and attempts to set up a dialectic discord between diverse artistic approaches. In seeking to address the nature and obligations of working within the art of the past and collections, other men's flowers asks what are the responsibilities to context when bringing such a disparate group of works together? What useful histories can unfold; How might we usefully understand the gaps and discrepancies in art production and dissemination?
>
> The exhibition is less concerned with histories of representation and illusion than it is with the lived experience or intervention offered by the work of art and how do artists deal with this experience as it somehow transforms their own field of vision."

Not exactly enlightened by this gobbledegook, I found that the works on show, by living Irish and foreign artists, were mostly of the kind called 'conceptual'. Rather than visual pleasure, they presented mental conceits, sights to puzzle over or to find quirkily clever (Klee and Dalí did the like ages ago). The works of one artist belonged to no category known to me: they were framed photographs of the backs of masterpieces by well-known Irish artists.

Sorting Out Art in Dublin

What is the Hugh Lane Gallery up to? Where is it heading? The collection of Irish, French and English paintings from around 1860 to 1908 with which it began was reasonably described as 'Modern Art', although it lacked representation of important new elements of that movement which were then emerging. In subsequent years, the Gallery added mainly new Irish paintings along with works from a wide variety of countries. The result was a collection notable principally as representing Irish painting during the period when, historically speaking, it first achieved a substantial collective existence. Most of it, as it happened, was contemporary with, and participated in, the movement of European painting known as 'Modern'. Then, in 2002, the Gallery dropped 'Modern' from its name, becoming simply Dublin City Gallery. The Hugh Lane. And around that time, or some years previously, its directing authority – its Board? - decided that 'Modern Art' (although still only very partially represented) was too limiting; it must venture also into that amorphous field of art which has followed the 'Modern' and is termed 'Contemporary, 'Followed the Modern'? Yes, all cultural movements called 'modern' or 'new' in their time come to an end but retain those given names in cultural history. Compare, in the 'medieval' fourteenth century, the *via moderna* (modern way) in philosophy, the *devotio moderna* in spirituality and the *ars nova* (new art) in music.

The Gallery's website now informs the world that it 'houses one of Ireland's foremost collections of modern and contemporary art.' 'The original collection…', it continues, 'has now grown to include almost 2000 artworks, ranging from the Impressionist masterpieces of Manet, Monet, Renoir and Degas to works by leading national and international contemporary artists'.

The disproportionate accommodation for Bacon and Scully, together with the *'other men's flowers'* exhibition, seem to show the direction in which the Gallery is now heading. The trouble is that this new element clashes with the historic nature and identity of the Gallery without indicating a coherent new identity. Somewhat like the European Union spreading from its historically grounded core in Western Europe into Eastern Europe, and eyeing territories beyond that, it seems to indicate an institution that has lost the run of itself.

It is normal for a public art gallery or museum to possess, by reason of its collection, a recognisable, differentiating identity. It possesses this distinctive identity in the context of similar institutions; the context being both international and, more particularly, that of the country or city where it is situated. Has the Dublin City Gallery. The Hugh Lane (an odd name when one comes to think of it) given thought to distinguishing itself from the Irish Museum of Modern Art, situated since 1991 also in Dublin? That museum's website informs the world that it 'was established by the Government of Ireland in 1990 as Ireland's first national institution for the presentation and collection of modern and contemporary art.' And it states further that 'the Irish Museum of Modern Art is Ireland's leading national institution for the collection and presentation of modern and contemporary art'.

When the Dublin City Gallery decided to re-present itself as housing 'one of Ireland's foremost collections of modern and contemporary art', it was aware that the IMMA, as it is usually called, was presenting itself in the terms I have just quoted. To be more specific, it was aware, when with fanfares it inaugurated its 'Scully Room', that the IMMA already housed Scully!

But now, to move on, what is one to think of the fact that the IMMA, which includes 'Modern' in its title, does not in practice even purport to be exhibiting 'Modern Art', in the concrete, historical sense of that term. Its website states: 'The Museum's acquisitions policy is to concentrate on the work of living artists, but it accepts donations ...with a particular emphasis on work from the 1940s onwards.' It is thereby in fact stating that it has been misnamed: that it should more correctly be called 'The Irish Museum of Contemporary Art'! And the fact is that what it exhibits, both from its own collection and in passing exhibitions, consists almost exclusively of the kind of art that – first in America, later also in Europe – followed the culmination of Modern Art with Jackson Pollock in the 1950s.[2] I mean that multiform kind of artistic production, mainly led and inspired by American artists, which I would term 'Whimsy Art'. I say 'whimsy' in the same, merely denominating sense as we use 'folly' to denote a certain historical kind of architecture. Apart from being a fair, comprehensive description of the many kinds of new work that have figured in museums and at art auctions since the late 1950s, it has an advantage as a name over 'Contemporary Art'. It does not require museums such as the IMMA to remove works from its walls or floors when a 'living artist' dies.

---

[2] In Europe, including Ireland, 'Modern Art', in forms preceding Jackson Pollock, continued to flourish through the 1960s.

To complete this sketch of the immediate, Dublin context in which The Dublin City Gallery. The Hugh Lane – and indeed the IMMA – exist, I add the self-definition of a third and very important Dublin art institution: The National Gallery of Ireland. Its website informs the world that it 'houses the national collection of Irish art and European master paintings'. Refining on that, it states that it is 'devoted to the collection and care of fine art dating it from c1300-c1950' and that its holdings 'include masterpieces by many of the most celebrated figures in the history of western European art from the Middle Ages *to the twenty-first century, including the most representative collection of historic Irish art.*' (Italics mine.)

'Western European art', whether 'to 1950' or 'to the twenty-first century' would of necessity include Modern Art. And when did or does 'historic Irish art' end?

In passing, it occurs to me – and this may reflect the present blurred mental state of the Dublin City Gallery – that of the three institutions it alone omits to state any date or dates to indicate the range of its collection. But the main point emerging from this sketch of Dublin's gallery situation must by now be more than obvious. The distribution of art works as between the three institutions urgently needs sorting out. For two reasons: for the sake of the mental coherence, dignity and grounded self-esteem of each institution, and for the guidance and pleasure of the art-loving public, native and from abroad. Such people like to find in a capital city a variety of public art galleries, and to know in which of them they can best view a particular kind or period of art. They like to know this, with reasonable accuracy, from the self-descriptions of the galleries – and then to find these self-descriptions verified when they visit one or other of them.

With regard in particular to the Gallery founded by Hugh Lane, and situated on Parnell Square, Dubliners would like to find it retaining, and building on, its original and well-loved character, however this may be defined.

IRISH TIMES AND IRISH PEOPLE

Saturday 7 June
Today *The Irish Times* published the following editorial under the heading *Are we out of our minds?* It begins:

> "ARE WE out of our collective minds? We are not going to win our money on 'the horses' if we say No to the Lisbon Treaty. We bought that nag in the last general election and, yet, here we go again. The latest *Irish Times*/TNSmrbi opinion poll suggests that we are set to reject the treaty in next Thursday's referendum. It is difficult to decipher why we would make such a short-sighted decision."

'And yet,' it continues, 'there is a strange public mood out there that is anti-establishment, anti-authority and anti-politician at this time'. A fair summary of the fears and annoyances that are moving people towards a No vote follows. It concludes with:

> "The economy is on a downward spiral. Jobs are threatened. And we were never told about the horses last year. These are all serious matters but they don't address the merits of the Lisbon Treaty. We would be wrong, so wrong, to use these irritating issues as a reason to vote No."

The argument for a Yes vote follows. Eccentrically for an editorial, it twice makes use of the imperative mood:

> "*Do not forget* that the formation of the original European Economic Community is the biggest peace project of the 20th century... *Remember* that our decision to join in 1973 was the most liberating action taken by this independent State setting us on the way to reversing the Act of Union, We moved out from the shadow of Britain for the first time and established our own identity. We took our place among the nations of the world with an influential voice. At a time when food and fuel prices are increasing and the global economic recession... now, more than ever, we must take a long-term rational view." *(Italics mine.)*

This is one of those rare editorials where *The Irish Times* shows its colours recklessly and passionately. The key features of the outburst are, first, the false 'we', recurring in the title and first paragraph, that actually stands for 'they, the Irish out there, the irrational *Irish* Irish – nationalists, Catholics, voters for Fianna Fáil, GAA players and so on'. In contrast to the conventional meaning of an editorial *we*, as a first person plural referring proudly to the collective formed by the newspaper's personnel, the 'we' used editorially here refers to a collective from which *The Irish Times* is proudly distant. It is at this lot that the two brusque imperatives are directed. Second, there is the implicit audience that is being mainly addressed, the paper's core public. This is the wealthy middle and upper middle class of what used to be called Dublin 4 (a postal district) and is now usually referred to as South Dublin (the constituencies of Dublin Southeast, Dublin South and Dún Laoghaire). Third, and occasioned by awareness of the irrational Irishry 'out there', there is the exasperated, hectoring tone, recalling the old Protestant Ascendancy tones of a huffing, puffing army major. And finally, there is the implication throughout that this is Reason countering ignorant instinct.

The passion, apart from expressing itself in those features, also comes through in the barely intelligible 'horse' sneers at the start and in a subsequent, incoherent paragraph. These refer to evidence given a few days ago to the Mahon Tribunal by the former taoiseach, Bertie Ahern. Asked to explain the origin of eight thousand pounds he had acquired on some date in the early 1990s, he said he had won it on the horses. But in the cases of 'we bought that nag in the last general election' and 'we were never told about the horses last year', the sneer has a dual target. Besides being directed at Bertie Ahern, it is directed at Fianna Fáil, the party of which he is leader. Consistently winning most electoral support and now the principal party in government, it is unanimously and oddly – but Reason when it gets passionate can assail odd targets – calling for a Yes vote in the referendum!

Immediately it recalled to my mind another *Irish Times* editorial of last autumn entitled 'A Poor Reflection of Ourselves' (I filed it) where the first person plural had the same connotation as in today's. At the time it evoked much shocked or amused comment for its naked scolding of the Irishry. It began:

> "WHAT SORT of people are we? We know now. The findings of the latest *Irish Times*/TNSmrbi opinion poll show that two out of every three voters believe that Bertie Ahern was wrong to accept €50,000 from his friends while he was minister for finance in 1993. He was also wrong to accept £8,000 sterling from the Manchester function in 1994.
>
> And yet, the Taoiseach, Mr Ahern, has increased his satisfaction rating by one percentage point to 53 per cent, the highest of all party leaders. More dramatically, Fianna Fáil support has received a huge boost. It is up eight percentage points since the last *Irish Times* poll in May. Support for Fianna Fáil has reached its highest level – 39 per cent – since the last general election.

What a paradox! The electorate, it appears, after 10 years of tribunals into various forms of corrupt payments, can set up a glass wall between this Taoiseach and Fianna Fáil, to distinguish between £8K from friends as distinct from £8 million to his mentor, Charles Haughey....
The culture of nods and winks and looking the other way is alive and well in Irish democracy... If the rest of us 'look the other way', it won't be long before the culture of corruption engendered by Mr Haughey will resurface. But, regrettably, this poll would indicate that this does not seem to matter..."

In the eyes of *The Irish Times* 'we', the electorate, the Irish, disgraced ourselves then, and are now, in this referendum, on the verge of doing so again. What is to be done? If *The Irish Times*, and that South Dublin – with affiliates elsewhere in the Republic – which it cossets by nod and wink are to be satisfied, then another, improved Irish people must urgently be found.

Perhaps there is some other ex-colonial country where the leading newspaper dissociates itself emotionally from the bulk of the nation and fosters a similarly alienated minority of well-off citizens. Perhaps, indeed, every modern nation carries within itself, and keeps reproducing in new terms, a socio-psychological structure acquired a few centuries ago. Certainly it is a fact that in eighteenth-century Ireland, and with less force in the following century, there was the so-called Protestant or Anglo-Irish Ascendancy, centred in Dublin but with attachments throughout the country, and emotionally more attached to England than to nationalist Ireland. Its members felt themselves mentally and morally superior to the Irish, specifically the Catholic Irish. In the nineteenth century it was 'unionist' in support of the political union with Britain. And, from the 1870s, as it so happens, this Ascendancy counted among its press organs *The Irish Times*: Protestant unionist, anti-nationalist, and of course opposed to the Revolution.

Adapting bravely but with great difficulty to the new scene after Independence, the paper's circulation fell to near vanishing point – until the early 1960s. Restoration of health arrived from the USA via London. It arrived in the form of that all-conquering left-liberal wave of the 1960s and the following decade which had, in-built in its mindset, a superior contempt for 'most people'; in the USA to begin with, but transferable at will. Cannily, *The Irish Times* mounted and rode that wave, adapting it to Ireland, and has since then never looked back. In tandem with the Dublin television station that started off in 1962, it developed, first in Dublin then more widely, a core adherence to the new liberalism. In the 1970s, as the rest of the Dublin media swung into line, and the cohort of converts widened, the *Times* became the house organ of the Irish liberal Correctorate. In that role, while remaining strongly seconded by RTÉ, it was the main driving force of what was called – in matters of contraception, divorce, homosexuality, abortion, historical revisionism and so on– 'the liberal agenda'.

From the start of its new departure, *The Irish Times* slotted – unconsciously I am sure, but perhaps because the Irish collective psyche required it – into something like the stance and role of its Protestant unionist predecessor. The in-built superiority complex of the paper's new liberalism played a notable part. A core element of its preaching was to the effect that 'we' must become 'outward-looking', which translated meant switch to regarding London as a benign influence rather than, as previously, a malign or suspect one. Along with this went early revisionist hints to the effect that perhaps 1916 and all that had been not entirely a good thing.[1] Then from 1973 onwards, after our accession to the European Community, the paper's attachment to London was largely replaced by a devoted adhesion to whatever Brussels decided or decreed for us.

That the Irish were not themselves capable of generating a satisfactory life – that a home-made Irish life was necessarily a malign thing – and that we were therefore in dire need of improvement from outside, was the underlying driving principle, now as a century previously. Then the needed improvement had been of the British liberal and Protestant kind (Victorian, in a word); now it was to be of the American left-liberal order. Once Brussels had been transatlantically *gleichgeschaltet*, and had in 1973 acquired a certain legal authority over us, it became logical to look to it rather than to London for such improvement. So in effect *The Irish Times* substituted for the pragmatic political unionism of the Irish electorate *vis-à-vis* Brussels an uncritical, ideologically-driven unionism.

---

[1] For a couple of examples of this incipient revisionism (not written, the then Editor told me, by himself), see my *Heresy: The Battle of Ideas in Ireland*, p.88. A complicating aspect of *The Irish Times* in those years was that the Editor leading the paper's new departure was Douglas Gageby, a traditional Wolfe Tone republican (and, as it happens, a good friend to me). Notoriously, in 1969, the British Ambassador in Dublin wrote in a letter to the British Foreign Office that, in conversation with an *Irish Times* director of the old school, Major McDowell, the latter spoke of Gageby as a 'white nigger'.

One aspect of this has been a harping retrospective devaluation of independent Ireland in the decades before its accession to the European Community, and in particular in the years prior to the *Irish Times*'s left-liberal enlightenment. Ireland was in those years – the paper's files since the 1960s will show – a dark, inward-looking, oppressively Catholic and de Valera place, with no achievement nor role in the world worth mentioning. And as it happens, in today's editorial, there is a striking example of such neo-unionist propaganda, partly dressed up in *faux* nationalist rhetoric. Here it is again:

> "Our decision to join [the European Community] in 1973 was the most liberating action taken by this independent State setting us on the way to reversing the Act of Union. We moved out from the shadow of Britain for the first time and established our own identity. We took our place among the nations of the world with an influential voice."

Spelt out – and ignoring the absurd hyperbole of 'the most liberating action, etc.' – that means that independent Ireland, by accepting a reduction in its sovereignty in exchange for benefits to be derived from a pooled sovereignty, began to end the *de facto* Act of Union with Great Britain which continued to exist after the Act itself had been legally abrogated. If understood in strictly economic terms, so far so good; but the argument then degenerates into a lying affront to the political history of independent Ireland.

When that Ireland, we are told, joined the European Community in 1973, we 'established our own [separate] identity for the first time and took our place among the nations of the world with an influential voice.' Actually, in sober historical fact, long before 1973, as independent Ireland, we had established our identity, separate from Britain's, and 'taken our place among the nations'. We had done so, first, as a member of the League of Nations in the 1930s and by means of the independent policy we pursued there; dramatically again, by remaining neutral in World War II while Britain fought; and in the 1950s and 60s, very notably, through our membership of the United Nations and the Council of Europe, and the independent foreign policy which the Republic pursued in those arenas. In the matter of having 'an influential voice among the nations', the Republic's sponsorship in the UN of the Nuclear Non-Proliferation Treaty, and its promotion of the admission of Communist China to that body, constitute a notable part of that organisation's history. Truly remarkable that the Irish 'newspaper of record' should, as a show of blind devotion to the European Union, engage in this suave erasure of independent Ireland's self-assertion among the nations *before its ability so to do was limited by accession to the European enterprise.*

Since the late 1960s, the notion that the Irish needed improvement effected by some foreign influence has not been peculiar to *The Irish Times*. The paper made, as I said, a growing corps of converts to its new liberalism; and the essential inadequacy of the Irish, or rather of the bulk of them, was a basic tenet of that creed. For a variety of reasons, mainly professional, the converts came to be concentrated in South Dublin.

That part of the Dublin suburbs was also, as it happened, home to the largest local Protestant minority in the Republic. But from the boom of the 1960s onwards, it was mainly new-rich Catholics who settled there. Well-off, many of them of rural origin and well-educated, they were acquainted with Swinging London, holidayed in France and Spain and farther afield, and felt attracted both to the progressive ideas and innovations of the Second Vatican Council and to the new liberalism. Accordingly, they came to feel themselves vaguely alienated from the more traditional inhabitants of the Republic and vaguely superior to them. They tended to read *The Irish Times* because, among Irish newspapers, it was the one considered somewhat alien, intellectual and posh (in most of the Republic it was believed to be a British paper). The renascent *Irish Times* met their psychological need in two ways. It gave them, by way of their assent to the paper's new liberal doctrines, concrete grounds for their superior feeling. In particular, it supplied the incontrovertible ground by building up over the years a derogatory profile of the inferior majority 'out there'.[2]

Above, in a few words, I adumbrated that derogatory profile. More expansively, in its finished, multi-layered form, it was 'inhabitants of a dark, traditional region called "rural Ireland" [connoting the Republic outside Dublin-south-of-the-Liffey]; Catholics attentive to their priests and averse to enlightened, liberal ideas and

---

[2] A collection of my *Sunday Press* columns, *Nice People and Rednecks*, published in 1986, dealt in part with this socio-ideological caricature, in the production of which *The Irish Times* played the leading, but not the only role. The 'Rednecks' of the title was drawn from its main secondary workshop, Dublin television. The station's in-house nickname for the daily programme that covered provincial news and events was 'Redneck Round-up' – a verbal illustration of how the snobbish American-liberal view of 'most people' had been superimposed on the old Protestant Ascendancy view.

laws, who regard all sex among adults as sinful or shameful; irrational, uncultured, dodgy people, lacking style, given to a fanciful nationalist, anti-English view of Irish history, and prone to sympathy with Republican violence; voters, most of them for Fianna Fáil, a party which produces governments riddled with corruption.'

Such, spelt out, is the 'Irish people' which *The Irish Times* has in mind in those two editorials: today's 'Are we out of our minds' and, some months ago, 'What sort of people are we?'. Such people are obviously in need of the kind of improvement which the enlightened 25,000 Brussels bureaucrats have been giving them, and will continue to give them if only they can be hectored into voting Yes. If they fail to do so, we – here a genuine, pally 'we' – are condemned to living on this island with them, cut off from civilisation. That is the essential subtextual message of today's editorial; and on its sentiments South Dubliners and their affiliates are largely in agreement with their mentor. They know that it is not they that the *The Irish Times* is hectoring.

Inasmuch as the argument for Yes in today's editorial is essentially on civilisational grounds it is, I think, unique in this referendum campaign. But given the anti-Establishment mood that is rampant on the No side – and to which indeed the editorial refers–it is not likely to have the effect desired. On the contrary, insofar as the Irishry out there read it, and feel its tone stirring unpleasant atavistic memories– as of hearing from the kitchen the landlord ranting in the drawing-room – it is likely to have the opposite effect. Which is not to say yet that the Noes have it. We shall see.

Dundrum's New Cathedral

Monday 9 June
My cottage in Dundrum in the 1960s stood across the Churchtown Road from St Nahi's church and graveyard. St Nahi's little church looked ancient, so it was no surprise for me to discover that the original church there had been eighth-century and built to honour a local saint. The present, ancient-looking Church of Ireland church was built a thousand years later, sometime in the eighteenth century. The old church had given the place its original name, Tigh Nathi (Nathi's House) which was then corrupted to Ti Nai and anglicised to Taney. Hence Taney Road, still in the locality today.

In the thirteenth century, when the English built a fort on a height to defend the Pale against the O'Byrnes and O'Tooles, Dundrum, Dún Droma (Ridge Fort), took over as the name. In the 1960s, when I lived there, it was a village consisting essentially of a main street which coincided with the road to Enniskerry. Still very much, in the feel of the place, outside Dublin four miles away, it acquired its first new housing estate during my years there. I married there and had my firstborn there. When in 1968 the authorities wanted to demolish our rented cottage to widen the Churchtown Road – a sign of what was coming and already happening – we moved to distant Conamara. Since then, Dundrum, or what in an expanded sense they call Dundrum, has grown and grown without me.

The culmination a few years ago – I heard of it in Italy – has been a spectacular shopping centre, the largest in Ireland, if not the world! Last year it won the European Award of the International Council of Shopping Centres. For the third year running it has won the top Irish prize for shopping centres. Called formally and a tad overbearingly Dundrum Town Centre, it has also been ironically referred to as 'Dundrum Cathedral'. Since I came back to Ireland, around the time that by general agreement the Celtic Tiger died, I have lamented that during those boom years some of the abundant money was not used to build anything splendid. Like anyone, I like splendour, and just as I believe with Aristotle that the rich man owes it to himself and others to practise magnificence, so, too, do I believe that any country, if it becomes rich, owes it to itself and the world to erect at least one new building that the world finds *splendid*. So it seemed to me that this

Dundrum phenomenon was worth inspecting.

Not only because it got that 'Cathedral' tag, Sunday seemed to be the day to visit it. That is the day of the week that large numbers of Dubliners now sanctify by a weekly shopping. Mel, who had been there and done that, said she would drive me there and leave me to my tourism while she did some shopping. As we approached what had been an old railway bridge at the lower end of Dundrum's main street, disorientation set in. A very tall concrete pylon, with a spread of steel girders descending at angles from it, reared up incongruously against the sky. It appeared, as we drew nearer, to be holding aloft a new, Luas bridge that crosses the road where the old railway bridge had been. Near where Churchtown Road veers off to the right, a new road with new housing had also taken off.

On the right-hand side of the rising main street as we drove up it, first a stretched-out two-storey building in rickety 1960s style flanked us, announcing itself as Dundrum Shopping Centre It, too, was doubtless a sensation in its day. Then came a line of ramshackle shopfronts and the fine neo-gothic stone church where my firstborn was baptised. At the top, to the right, a tall new building consisting of blocky shapes of various materials and colours loomed. I took it to be the new shopping centre, in the style of those architectures which show their best face inward. Beside it, up steps, was a broad entrance from the footpath to what looked like a sort of plaza. We passed it to find the attached car park which turned out to be four levels high.

As we entered its ground level, alienation seized me and hung in the air. In the dim light hundreds of cars covered an area the size of two football fields. We parked there, and as we left the car noticed that a little red light had come on above it. There were similar red lights above the other cars, but a green light where there was still a space. Useful, I thought, as we found a pedestrian exit direct into the shopping centre, Level 1.

It presented itself as a very wide, tiled and covered street – mall, I suppose they say – filled with many people in easy movement. The tiles were large, glossy, beige, and made a fine surface. We passed some big, illuminated shop-windows showing men's and women's clothes. Zara, Pamela Scott, Massimo Dutti; Clarkes for shoes. Two couples strolled hand in hand, glancing sideways, as if walking in a park or visiting a zoo. Hearing Polish spoken confirmed that we were in Dublin or near it. Glancing down a side-passage I noticed a series of large wall charts. Because they seemed to be offering information about the Centre, I agreed with Mel that we would meet again there in exactly two hours time and she departed. Over the charts or display boards there was a large heading: 'Evolution from Village to Town Centre'. I went to the first board in order, and settled down to read and make notes.

A corn mill, the story began, is known to have existed here in 1602. In the nineteenth century there was a mill pond fed by the River Slang. In 2001, site work for Dundrum Town Centre Shopping Centre began with 'major excavation work'. This included the removal of 300,000 cubic metres of granite, mostly by blasting at a rate of three major blasts each week for more than a year, with up to 300 charges per blast.

Concrete used in the construction amounted to 100,000 m^3. Steel used, 27,000 tonnes. Overburden, 220,000 m^3. Blockwork, 65,000 m^2. Partitions, 15000 m^2. Envelope, 20,000 m^2. Stair cores, 46. Lifts, 30. Doors, 1000. Light fittings, 6000. Height 53.5m (175ft). River suspended within building for 100m.

First stage of the DTC opened March 2005. 90,000 m^2 retail space. Car spaces, 3400. 400 CCTV cameras. More than six million visitors in first 6 months.

I returned to the broad tiled mall where dark green tiles were making patterns amid the beige. Back in the direction from which I had come, two lines of people moved past each other on escalators in what seemed to be the Penney's and Marks and Spencer's sector. Continuing in the direction I had been going, I saw a space widening out ahead. A long counter there announced itself as a Butler's café offering Butler's chocolates, my favourites and without doubt the best in the world. Reassured by this encounter, I felt the alienation that had descended in the car park lift. Equipped with a little bag of dark chocolate delights and a large carton of coffee, I proceeded towards what looked like an even larger open space bathed in sunlight. Past Weir's jewellery, Molton Brown's soaps, and L'Occitane en Provence, I reached it.

It was indeed a large open space bathed in sunlight, with low buildings around it and in the centre a roughly rectangular pond. Here and there on its surface, slender jets rose and fell and there was also a ring of them. A small notice on the surrounding railing said 'Mill Pond'. It informed me that the water was from the River Slang, which had supplied water to a millstream that once turned the wheels of an ironworks. Searching for a bench, I saw instead, around circles of shrubs each with a tree at its centre, low squat walls cladded in check-pattern mosaic. People were sitting on them. A large television screen was relaying a football match. At some distance to the right, I spied what looked like Dundrum main street, and approaching it, found that it was indeed that. I was back at that entrance from the footpath which I had noticed from the car. So this, I realised, was the proper approach to the shopping centre, and I had entered by, so to speak, a back door.

Turning around, I readjusted my perspective, as if entering from the street. In front of me now, what I presumed was the 'town square' of this mini-town which the shopping centre purported to be; a town square laid out around a pond;bordered, I now saw, by tall green reeds. To my left, up some steps, the black entrance to a cinema showing Ocean's 13. In there, some lettering indicated, a McDonald's, a Kentucky Chicken, an Eddie Rocketts and a Pizza Hut might also be found.To my right, beyond the near end of the pond, the beige Mill Theatre. Until 31 May it had had Martin McDonagh's *Beauty Queen of Leenane*; from the 13th it would have *The Wonderful World of Dissocia* by Anthony Nielson.

The plaza was paved with beige tiles. There seems to have been an opting for beige in various shades and brownish colours as the Centre's predominant colouring. To finish my coffee, I sit on one of the low, check-patterned walls, facing the pond. The two girls beside me are speaking Spanish. On the far railing, in case an urgent call for help might intrude on this tranquil scene, a lifebuoy hangs. Suddenly there are high spurts all over the pond; a sort of fireworks display of water, with momentary rainbows dancing through it. Then again suddenly, it is over. Beyond the pond people are sitting at tables under sun umbrellas in front of a two-storey café-restaurant. I am in the sunny south, somewhere Mediterranean. I am not. I am looking, to the left of the café, down a new street of empty shops that leads the eye to the rear part of the village church. That, a sign says, is to be the Pembroke District, opening in October. To the left of it, a high wall of dark glass forms the two-storey side of Harvey Nichols.

I rose and returned to the main building, entering this time by the proper main door, where House of Fraser declared its occupancy of two storeys. Back on the mall where I had started, and again passing Weir's, I see a woman standing at an information pillar with a computer screen. She is pressing the name *Accessorize* to locate that shop. Informed, she makes way for a young man who, inserting the registration number of his car – I assume it is his car – finds where it is located in the car parks. That must mean that, as you park, your registration number is photographed. At the foot of an escalator a signpost says Crèche, Gallery, Customer Service. The escalator has glass sides and a shiny black banister. As it carries me up, jutting away from the mall into the vast central space under the roof several levels higher, a couple with children are descending a broad two-flight staircase that similarly juts out, and then turns, in the same great space.

I am on Level 2 noting Accessorize, Monsoon for Children and Cassidy Travel. At the Customer Service counter a girl tells me that Sunday and Saturday are their busiest days, about 50,000 visitors on each day. Five thousand people work in the Centre. Exploring down a corridor towards Crèche and Baby Changing, I see through a wall of glass a broad paved terrace and mature trees. Light, artificial or flooding in from outside. makes brightness everywhere. The crèche is an open-sided room full of children's toys, with three children sitting among them. As I look, beyond the fat brown woman in charge, through more glass to the trees, she observes me apprehensively.

Up again, this time to Replay and Bertoni for Men. Is that mall full of people that I see down there the one I was on or another? No hope, as one moves through it all, of maintaining orientation. At a point where I can see two levels simultaneously, I stand and take stock. Three stable elements, one horizontal and two perpendicular, hold together the kaleidoscope of coloured shop fronts, moving escalators and multi-garbed people. They are the solid beige bulkheads that support the levels, the thick beige pillars of varying height that hold up ceilings, escalators and flights of stairs, and the polished red wood of the elevator tower that, with two cabins, ascends through all levels from bottom to top. All the colours of the bearing structure and of the shopfronts are fresh, all surfaces gleam clean; a staff of sweepers and polishers are continually at their modest work. It seems that this level I am on is called 'Gallery'. There are café tables along the railing that surrounds the central well, and on one of them, two chained laptops, apparently for the customers.

Up again, and I seem to be now as high as the escalators will take me. There are children's toys, mobile phone shops and an Eason's. The House of Fraser seems always to be present – I have seen it on every level, as if it rises though them. Backed by big windows, a sea of tables fills an immense eating area called, I gather, a 'food court'. To either side of it, counters with big signs: Pizzeria, Sandwich Bar, Coffee and Cake, Pasta, Carvery, Oriental. This Dundrum Town Centre, with its thirty eating places on three levels, is almost as much for eating as for shopping. And here I come on the first food shop (or rather, in the vernacular of the place, store) though there must surely be others. This oceanic Tesco's, extending away from me, has – I count, as I walk past – nineteen serviced checkouts and eight self-service ones. And it displays the solitary Irish word I have encountered: 'Slán. Thank you for shopping with us',

From here, I could travel higher by stairs or *elevator*, not of course *lift*, to Levels 4 and 5, where there are hairdressers, a beautician, a medical centre, adult education centre, citizens' information centre – even an RTÉ studio! The Dundrum Town Centre Shopping Centre does truly provide all that a self-respecting town or a human heart could desire, except an oratory. But I refrain from ascending further. I have seen, just past Tesco's, through ceiling-high glass, a great open-air car park and, beyond it, trees and houses. And I am amazed that these trees and houses seem to be almost on the level of the car park. It appears that as I rose through the building, this part of it was, so to speak, rising against a hillside, so that it can disgorge me here almost on ground level again.

Stepping into the car park, I see beyond and above the trees one of those modest green excrescences that we call the Dublin Mountains. I will not have their modesty mocked, I knew them well as a boy. That one straight ahead from me, with the communications masts on its summit, is Three Rock. Good to see you again, Three Rock. As for Dundrum Town Centre Shopping Centre, now behind me, and of which I have seen perhaps a half, well yes, it is a fitting memorial to the Celtic Tiger and, as shopping centres go, splendid.

THE NO TO LISBON

Friday 13 June
In yesterday's referendum on the Lisbon Treaty we voted No by a large majority, 53-46%. The biggest local majorities for the Yes vote were in the three constituencies which make up South Dublin; in each of them, over 60%.

*

An email arrived from Tim Campbell of the St Patrick Centre, Downpatrick. He has had a visit from some people from Ballycastle on the north coast of Co. Mayo. They believe that the Wood of Foclut was located somewhere around there and are wondering whether a St Patrick trail might link it with Downpatrick. That would be strategically important for my Slí Phádraig - linking the West through the North with Downpatrick. Tim showed them my map and sent me a photo of the group, with himself holding it up.

LOVE OF COUNTRY IS A RESOURCE IN HARD TIMES

Postscript November 2008

Squirrels are wise. In autumn they bury nuts to live on in the winter months. Nations are similarly wise when they stock up on love of country. It nourishes them emotionally when, because of war, famine or economic downturn, times become hard.

Put more precisely, nations are fortunate when their public figures – political leaders, poets, writers, historians, commentators – display love of country. This display of it evokes it and develops it in the nation, thereby making that nation self-loving; hard times more bearable; and morale despite hardship high.

In the media coverage of the American presidential campaign over many months, a striking feature was the frequent expression of love of country by the leading actors. 'God bless America', 'I love America', 'this great nation', 'land of the free', 'to make America again a beacon for the world' – such were the recurrent public declarations. That America for the speakers was something precious, and therefore lovable and to be loved, was not only evident to us bystanders; primarily it was an exhortation to the applauding thousands to participate in the declared love.

In this respect, America is fortunate as it faces into hard times. Its self-love is secure against those domestic critical voices which assert, often on good grounds, that one or other aspect of America is abhorrent. Its nationalism, in the basic sense of love and celebration of one's nation, is strong enough to prevail.

In Europe the case is different. From the start of the united-Europe enterprise, the message of its leaders has been that Europe's nationalisms were to be superseded by an emotional commitment to Europe. The competing nationalisms of the nations were declared an obstacle to be removed. And accordingly, in the various nations – with varying degrees of thoroughness but everywhere with effect–the pro-European elites discouraged the felt love of country which had been proclaimed for centuries.

This might not have mattered if the constructors of united Europe, in their successive generations, had been lovers of Europe as distinct from lovers of their construct; if, that is, they had been lovers of actual inherited and living Europe who, moreover, proclaimed that love credibly, articulated grounds for it and educated the member nations into it, so that Europe came to be for all of us, emotionally, our new, great over-arching nation. I mean to say, came to be for all of us something like what America is for Americans, China for the Chinese, and Russia for the Russians.

But none of that happened. After, to be precise, the first generation, the constructors of united Europe loved only their construct. The peoples of Europe called that construct 'Brussels' and their feelings towards it boiled down to three. It was often a useful source of cash, often an irritating intruder in their lives, and sometimes an effective asserter of rights which their national governments denied them. But of love, not the slightest trace.

Meanwhile, inside the member nations, love of country had become, in varying degrees, 'the love that dare not speak its name'. The national elites whom Brussels had encouraged to suppress it had more or less succeeded. In Ireland their success was great; greater than in any other member-state except Germany. When did we last hear or read an Irish public figure declaring 'I love Ireland, this precious land'?

The most effective way to suppress love of country in present-day Europe is to conduct a national media campaign which declares the nation to be, for a variety of reasons, *unlovable*; to be a nation which requires, for its life to be even ordinarily adequate, the improving influences of favoured foreign nations or of the bureaucrats in Brussels.

This campaign must consist of more than the writings and utterances of journalists: it must also, to drive the 'unlovable' message home, provide privileged platforms for all those who hold this view or who write books, or make speeches, proclaiming this view.

For the past forty years we have seen such a campaign conducted by the mass media in this Republic, under the joint leadership and inspiration of *The Irish Times* and the national broadcaster RTÉ. The effect here, as it would be similarly elsewhere, has been to intimidate – it is a strategy of 'shock and awe' – those who would otherwise have continued that public declaration of love of Ireland which previously came naturally to the Irish: as *Gaeilge* for 1400 years, in English for 300. They were intimidated into silence.

This explains why the public sounds during the hard times ahead will consist only of raucous complaint, cries of injustice done, and tales of inflicted misery on radio and television – all of it depressing our national morale and awakening desires to emigrate.

Afterthought

It has occurred to me that the West's rejection of western civilisation might not preclude a return to it. Have there been previously such rejections followed by returns? I have been investigating the Black Death and the so-called Intermediary Periods of ancient Egyptian civilisation. In the Black Death 40-50 per cent of the European population are reckoned to have died in four years. That caused great social upheaval, disorganisation and anguish, but no lasting rejection of the inherited values and rules. Apart from inessential adjustments, mainly in the economic field, these continued to hold good when, remarkably, life resumed its course a few years later.

As for the Intermediate Periods in Egyptian civilisation, well, they turn out to be indeed that – periods within the course of that same civilisation. They were three periods when the centralised pharaonic government ceased to function, and a variety of local powers, sometimes including foreign intruders, replaced it.

It occurs to me that there was actually here in Ireland a previous occasion when, under devastating foreign pressure, we rejected our local inherited civilisation and never returned to it. I mean, of course, that in the sixteenth and seventeenth centuries we progressively and definitively rejected our Christian Gaelic civilisation – our particular, home-made version of European civilisation. Beginning in the eighteenth century, we replaced that with a Catholic English version a l'irlandaise *of the same civilisation. Which we have now left.*

INDEX

Afghanistan 22
Africa 27
Ahern, Bertie 30
American Congress 30
American Declaration of Independence 12
Asia 27
Assumption 61
Athol Books 9
Atomic bomb 12
Augher 53

Bacon, Francis 79
Ballina 53
Belvedere College 78
Big State 12
Black Death 100
Bono 28
Boole 14
Boyne 30
Brussels 32,38
Bucharest 35
Buckley, William 41,
Budapest 27
Bush, George 66
Byelorussia 55

Camino de Santiago 51
Campbell, Tim 51,97
Camus 5
Canada 54,55
Celtic Tiger 41,91
Chad 57
China 25,57
Christian morality 20
Church & State 8
Civil Rights 13
Civilisation, what is. 10
Clara 30
Claremorris 52
Clarke, Harry 79
Clew Bay 52
Clonmell House 78
Cold War 34,35
Collins 42

Collooney 53
Colton, E.T, 8
Columbia 22
Communism 32
Corinthians 67
Correctorate, the Liberal. 15,16,20,21,24,37,39,48
Courbet 79
Cowen, Brian 5,30,33,
Croaghpatrick 52
Cuchulainn 43,44,

'Dawn chorus' 34,
Data Protection Commissioner 36,
de Tocqueville 37,76
de Valera 42
Denmark 31,33
Donegal 52
Down, Co. 79
Downpatrick 51,53,97
Dromore 53
Dublin City Gallery 83
Dublin Municipal Gallery 78
Dundrum 91-96

Easter Fire 52
Egypt 36,100
ENP 54
Ephesians 67
European Union 54-59
Evil 35,

Father Matthew 43
Flannery, Austin, Fr. 63

Gaeilge 33
Gaeltacht 5
Gageby, Douglas 87
Galway 79
Gandon 73
Ganley, Declan 70
Georgia 55
German Revolution

8,9,15
Good 35
GPO 41,42,44,
Gray, Sir John 44
Great Depression 12
Greece 55,73

Haughey Charlie 71
Hawkwes, Mr. 36
Home-Rule 31
Hungary 33
Hyde, Douglas 42

'Irish Mind, The' 28,
Irish Museum of Mod. Art 82
Irish Political Review 10
Irish Revolution 31,33
Irish State 31
Irish Times 35,60,63, 84-90
Italy 5,8,10,12,61,62

Jacobins 36
Japan 12,57
Johnson, Pres. 14

Kant 14
Kavanagh, Patrick 44,
Kazakhstan 55
Keane, Terry 71-4
Kilalla 52
King's College 54

l'Osservatore Romano 62
Laidler, Keith 35
Lane, Hugh, Sir, Gallery 78,80,81
Laogaire, High King 52
Larkin, James 42, 43, 44
Lemass 42
Lenihan, Brian 58
Libertas 70
Libya 57
Lisbon Treaty 58,69-70,97
Lithuania 39

101

Littleton, John 60
Liturgy Commission 66
Lough Derg 52
Lynch, Dov 54, 55

Magris, Claudio 36,
Maher, Eamon 60
Manet 79
Martin, Diarmaid 63
Marx 14
Maynooth 34
McCreevy, Charlie 69
McDowell, Major 87
Melvin, Lough 53
Minerva Press 9
Mondrian 80
Moscow 34
Mozart 14
Mussolini 10,11,12

Native Americans 23
NATO 55
Netherlands 33
New Deal 11,13
Newton 14
Nixon, Pres. 14
Norway 31

O'Brien, William Smith 44
O'Casey, Sean 44
O'Connell St. 41,42,43
O'Connell, Daniel 11
Offaly 30

Opie, Julian 43
Orwell, George 34
OSCE 54

Padre Pio 62
Paisley, Ian 30
Pakenham, Judith 17
Parnell Monument 43
Partisan Review 14
Pascal 14
Phoenix 6
Pollock, Jackson 82
Post-Europe 29
Prague 35

'Redneck round-up' 89
Referendum
   Commission 75
Roman Empire 8,22,25
Roosevelt, F.D,11
RTE 35
Russia 57
Russian Revolution
   8,9,12,15,22,23

St. Matthew 67
Shakespeare 14
Sontag, Susan 14
'Spire, The' 41, 44
Sweden 31,64
St. Patrick's Day 61
St. Patrick's Way 51,97
Slane, Hill of. 52

Slemish 52
South Caucuses 54
Symes, R. 8
Stations of the Cross 65
Second American
   Revolution 7,8,9,29, 37
San Francisco 19,27

Tara 52
Thessalonians 67
Totalitarianism 34-36
Treaty Ports 31
Truman years 13
Tullamore 30
Turkey 55
Twin Towers 34
Twomey, Vincent 61
Tyrone 53

Ukraine 55
Ulster Way 53
United Nations 20
US Supreme Court 14
USA 5,7,9,11,15,25,32,
   34,54

'White Nigger' 87
Waters, John 46-50
Westport 52
Wiggins, Maurice 17
Wolf, Naomi 19

Yeats 42

View a full list of publications
distributed by

ATHOL BOOKS

and order literature on

www.atholbooks.org